FLEETING OPPORTUNITIES

SUNY Series in American Labor History

Robert Asher and Charles Stephenson, Editors

FLEETING OPPORTUNITIES

*Women Shipyard Workers
in Portland and Vancouver
During World War II and Reconversion*

Amy Kesselman

STATE UNIVERSITY OF NEW YORK PRESS

Portions of this work were originally published as Chapter 13 in *Hidden Aspects of Women's Work*, Christine Bose, Roslyn Feldberg, and Natalie Sokoloff, Eds. (Praeger Publishers, New York, a division of Greenwood Press, 1987), pp. 283–298. Reprinted with Permission.

Published by
State University of New York Press, Albany

For information, address State University of New York
Press, State University Plaza, Albany, N.Y., 12246

Library of Congress Cataloging in Publication Data

Kesselman, Amy Vita, 1944-
    Fleeting opportunities : women shipyard workers in Portland and
Vancouver during World War II and reconversion / Amy Kesselman.
        p.   cm. – (Suny series in American labor history)
    Bibliography: p.
    Includes index.
    ISBN 0-7914-0174-X. – ISBN 0-7914-0175-8 (pbk.)
    1. Shipbuilding industry – Oregon – Portland – Employees – History.
2. Shipbuilding industry – Washington – Vancouver – History.   3. Women –
Employment – Oregon – Portland – History.   4. Women – Employment –
Washington – Vancouver – History.   5. Sex discrimination in
employment – Oregon – Portland – History.   6. Sex discrimination in
employment – Washington – Vancouver – History.   7. World War,
1939–1945 – Economic aspects – Oregon – Portland.   8. World War,
1939–1945 – Economic aspects – Washington – Vancouver.   I. Title.
II. Series.
HD6073.S52U64   1990
331.4'8238204'0979549 – dc19   89-4364
                                                                  CIP

10 9 8 7 6 5 4 3 2 1

For my parents, Ethel and Bernard Kesselman

CONTENTS

Tables

ACKNOWLEDGMENTS

Fleeting Opportunities emerged from the twin processes of writing a dissertation and collecting oral histories with the Northwest Women's History Project. I am grateful to the former shipyard workers who shared their memories and for their enthusiasm about documenting the history of women in the Portland and Vancouver shipyards. I would particularly like to thank Doris Avshalomov for permission to publish her poem, "Graveyard Shift, Vancouver Ship." Interviews of former shipyards workers were conducted by me and other members of the Northwest History Project: Sarah Cook, Susan Feldman, Barbara Gundle, Madeline Moore, Sandy Polishuk, Tina Tau, Lynn Taylor, Barbara Whittlesy-Hayes, and Karen Wickre, each of whom brought unique skills and perspectives to the project. I am grateful for their insights, and the many hours of volunteer labor involved in preparing for and collecting the oral histories which are central to this book. I would also like to thank Karen Beck Skold who shared materials with me and whose interviews with people connected with wartime child care were extremely helpful.

The dissertation upon which *Fleeting Opportunities* is based, was written at Cornell University, where it benefited from the thoughtful criticism of Mary Beth Norton, my dissertation advisor. I am also grateful for the helpful suggestions of Richard Polenberg, Sally McConnell-Ginet, Gale McGovern, and the members of the Women and Work study group.

Many friends and colleagues helped me shape the dissertation into a book. Robert Asher, Sherna Berger Gluck, Ruth Meyerowitz, Meredith Tax, John Wilhelm, and the reviewers for SUNY Press read the entire dissertation and made valuable suggestions. Rickie Solinger worked with me chapter by chapter, providing perceptive criticism along the way and much-needed clarity at several critical junctures. Susan Seyl of the Oregon Historical Society spent many hours tracking down photographs. The enthusiasm and support of Naomi Weisstein and Lee Ann Bell sustained me throughout the rewriting process.

My deepest appreciation goes to my friend Virginia Blaisdell who applied her critical intelligence, her editorial skill, and her intolerance for obfuscation to countless drafts of *Fleeting Opportunities*, enriching it immeasurably.

INTRODUCTION

"My fellow Americans. I ask your help. On behalf of all your fighting sons, brothers, and husbands whom I command in the Pacific, I ask that every skilled man and woman in American who can work in a shipyard volunteer immediately."

Admiral Chester W. Nimitz
Commander in Chief, U.S.
Pacific Fleet

In 1943, Joanne Hudlicky, a sales clerk at a cigar store in Vancouver, Washington, took a job in the clearance office of the huge shipyard that had just been built by the Kaiser Corporation in Vancouver, Washington. Attracted to the salaries of production workers, she transferred to the yards and eventually became a crane operator. For Hudlicky, a divorced mother, the shipyard wages promised some relief from the constant anxiety about making ends meet. Hudlicky enjoyed the physical challenge of crane operating–it evoked memories of her high school years as an athlete. After the war she remarried, had three children and, after her youngest child entered high school, worked at her mother's bar until retirement. Crane operating was the peak experience of Joanne Hudlicky's life. She felt that it was an ideal job for her because it was physically and mentally challenging and its appeal was enhanced by the knowledge that it was something women weren't supposed to do.[1]

Rosa Dickson and her husband left their farm in Texas and moved first to Arizona where Rosa had a part interest in a self-service laundry, and then to Portland where Mr. Dickson got a job in a shipyard. With three of her five children still at home, Rosa wanted to contribute to the family income and, recognizing that the best wages were at the shipyards, she took a job as a welder at Albina Engine and Machine Works, one of the older, smaller shipyards in the area. Finding the clothes too heavy and uncomfortable, Dickson became a pipe fitter's helper and continued in various helper jobs until 1946. With the wages they earned at the shipyard, the Dicksons were able to buy

1

the house they lived in for the rest of their lives. After the war Dickson worked in canneries and garment factories. Her feelings about the shipyards are mixed. Shipyard work had lifted them out of poverty and Dickson was proud of her contribution. A devout Baptist, she cites the Bible to support the validity of women working and exerting leadership outside the home, but she is troubled by the changes in social and sexual behavior that she says began in the shipyards.[2]

Beatrice Marshall, a college student in Illinois who wanted to help the war effort, was trained as a machinist in a National Youth Administration Program and sent to the Oregon shipyards. Because she was black, however, she was refused work as a machinist and hired as an unskilled laborer. Finding the laborer jobs dirty and tedious, she left the Portland area, first to work in Los Angeles and then to finish school in Illinois. She later returned to Portland and worked as a page in the public library. For Marshall, the training program was exciting, but the shipyard experience was one of bitter disappointment – her most painful encounter with racism.[3]

Rosa Dickson, Beatrice Marshall, and Joanne Hudlicky were three of the 40,000 women who worked in the shipyards on the banks of the Willamette and Columbia Rivers in Portland, Oregon, and Vancouver, Washington, during World War II. The meaning of war work for the thousands of women who worked in war industries – women who brought with them a variety of expectations and experiences – has been obscured for decades by the prevailing image of Rosie the Riveter reluctantly discarding her apron and, thinking tearfully of her menfolk in the service, joining the industrial workforce to do her bit. At the war's end, the story goes, she gratefully retired her work clothes and began having babies and buying appliances.

Recent research has called this image into question and suggests that the experiences of American women war workers were complex and varied. Like Joanne Hudlicky, more than half of the women who worked during World War II had been working before the war. The married women workers who joined the work force for the first time were part of a long-term trend that began before the war, and, like Rosa Dickson, many of the new women workers had been contributing to the family income in whatever way they could. While patriotism contributed to the motivation of some women war workers, most needed paid work and many were attracted to defense jobs by the high wages.[4] Government and industry courted women workers, but, as in the case of Beatrice Marshall, discrimination on the basis of race and sex often prevented women from fully contributing their skills to the war effort.[5] After the war, many women war workers, like Rosa Dickson, continued to work for wages and many, like Joanne Hudlicky and Beatrice Marshall, rejoined the work force soon after.[6] This new understanding of the history of wage-earning women makes the postwar fate of women war workers even more perplexing. The war opened doors in the industrial work force that had been previously closed to women, and wartime polls indicated that substantial numbers of women wanted to continue in their wartime occupations. In the context of the long-term trend towards more female labor force participation, the virtual disappearance of women from the skilled industrial work force after the war, the reestablishment of rigid sex segregation, and the post-war glorification of domesticity raise the question first asked by Sheila Tobias and Lisa Anderson in 1973, "What happened to Rosie the Riveter?" And, we might add, "Wanda the Welder" as well.

In the past ten years historians have found a partial answer to the question of women's post-war fate by investigating the wartime experience itself and discovering that the widened opportunities for women wage earners were accompanied by the uniform resistance of social institutions to any lasting change in the sexual division of labor. Research has demonstrated that while the wartime labor shortage created opportunities for women, lasting change was inhibited by the government, unions, and media, and management.[7] Even the rhetoric of the government recruitment drive communicated a double message to women: they should take on new challenges for the war effort but retain their primary identity as wives, girlfriends, and mothers.[8]

Several excellent studies have found reverberations of this double message throughout wartime society. It was reflected in the inadequate and conflict-ridden federal child-care program and the failure of the federal government and all but four states to go beyond rhetorical commitment to equal pay for equal work.[9] It was communicated through the reproduction of sex segregation in the work force; even as women entered what had previously been male territory, they were concentrated in certain jobs.[10] The work that women did was described in ways that rendered it consistent with traditional notions of femininity, thus reconciling "women's new economic situation with their traditional position as guardians of the hearth."[11]

Any permanent inroads by women into the industrial crafts would depend to a great extent on the attitudes of male workers and labor unions. Most unions failed to insist on equal pay for women and did not support women's seniority rights during demobilization.[12] As Ruth Milkman demonstrates in her incisive study of the automobile and electrical industries, the responses of male-dominated unions depended to a great extent on the structure of the industry and its prewar employment patterns. Women in both industries organized to defend their rights at the end of the war, but the unions responded differently. The United Auto Workers (UAW) did not support women's efforts to retain their seniority rights after the war, while the United Electrical Workers, fearing the effect of female substitution on men's wages, supported women's fight against a dual wage system. While in the long run, as Milkman notes, the class interests of male workers are not served by sex segregation, men have historically acted more frequently in defense of what she calls their "gender interests" and worked to preserve sex segregation than they have in defense of women's rights. While male workers did at times perceive common interests with female workers, this did not constitute a challenge to the sexual division of labor in the workplace and did not involve relinquishing gender-related privileges.[13]

These studies of government policy, media images, and the attitudes of unions have been extremely useful in explaining why World War II did not result in permanent improvement in the work lives of women wage earners. But while the forces that impeded women's progress during World War II emerge with clarity, women remain shadowy figures in much current scholarship, leaving unanswered questions about how women themselves saw their work situations and the options available to them.

A small but growing body of literature is addressing itself to the subject of women's consciousness during the 1940s. Andrea Walsh finds "nascent feminism" in the films of the 1940s, which she views as a "metaphorical avenue to the consciousness of American women."[14] The films that aimed at female audiences, Walsh argues, were based on the "assumption that women can make choices" and expressed a view of womanhood that was "strong, maternal and sisterly; desiring yet distrusting and angry towards men; excited about as well as ambivalent toward and frightened of independence and autonomy."[15] In contrast, D' Ann Campbell cautions against imposing the values of the 1970s and 1980s on the world of the 1940s and concludes that women participated reluctantly in the production effort and chose the family-centered world of the postwar period. The "strictly defined guidelines" within which people of the 1940s made choices, according to Campbell, "emerged from the people, particularly the women, who were charged with responsibility for guiding children to do the right and proper thing."[16] People of the 1940s, she argues, were "less sensitive to individual needs, aspirations and abilities and yet more sensitive to the private demands of family and the public demands made by the nation in the name of patriotism." According to Campbell, only a minority of women had "a taste for male jobs, or aspired to a rewarding career," a conclusion she reaches on the basis of the 1940s poll data.[17]

Broad-brush panoramas such as Campbell's can etch the contours of postwar values, which certainly glorified domesticity and denigrated female autonomy and ambition. But we need to get closer to women's experience to obtain any meaningful explanation of the genesis of these values and what they meant in women's lives. As Alice Kessler-Harris has pointed out, "Aspirations are themselves conditioned by perceptions of available opportunities."[18] A brief consideration of one of the three women who opened this chapter can illuminate the complexity of "taste" and "aspiration" and the ambiguity of poll data.

Joanne Hudlicky left the work force to raise her children after the war, and she reported "being very glad that I have a nice family." She thinks, however, if she "hadn't done that and had wanted to work longer," being unable to continue as a crane operator would have been a "disappointment." Watching women athletes on TV can still send chills down Hudlicky's spine, stimulating her to think about what she could have done if she had been able to continue in athletics as a young girl. How would she have answered in a poll in the 1940s? We don't know. She was happy with her family life and she may have become conscious of the ways she had adjusted to limited opportunities only when she reflected upon her life through the vantage point of the 1980s. Nevertheless, her reflections reveal the ways limited opportunities interacted in the lives of women to shape their choices, their expectations, and their values.[19]

Sherna Gluck, in her analysis of the oral histories of Los Angeles aircraft workers, offers an alternative view of the post-war glorification of domesticity, seeing it as a reaction to changes in women's attitudes.[20] "The unintended effect of their wartime experience" on the lives of the majority of aircraft workers she interviewed was "a transformation in their concept of themselves as women. This change," argues Gluck, "was not translated into a direct challenge of the status quo. At the time, it was probably not even recognized by most of the women, but it did affect their status in their own eyes – and in their homes."[21]

Fleeting Opportunities, a study of women industrial workers in the wartime shipyards of Vancouver, Washington, and Portland, Oregon, two adjacent communities on the Columbia River, is meant to be a contribution to this discussion. The assumption I bring to this study is that women, like men, seek ways to enrich their lives and that the form these efforts take is affected by the environment in which they live and work. Using a case study approach, which brings the researcher close to the texture of daily life, I have tried to reconstruct the dynamic generated by women attempting to shape their lives in an environment that sometimes presented them with opportunities and challenges and at other times with constraints and obstacles. *Fleeting Opportunities* will explore women's responses and their perceptions of the choices available to them in the context of various social, cultural and political influences.[22] Rather than presenting women's shipyard work as a discrete event, *Fleeting Opportunities* seeks to connect the wartime experience with both the prewar and postwar worlds.

Shipbuilding before World War II was a male preserve. Only 2 percent of the entire shipyard work force was female in 1939.[23] A Women's Bureau publication described the industry as "so thoroughly male that any woman who ventured into a yard was greeted with hooting and whistling."[24] The war, however, quickly transformed the shipbuilding industry, ushering in large numbers of new, hastily trained, inexperienced workers. By January 1944, between 10 and 20 percent of all shipyard production workers were women, many of whom were journeymen welders. After the war shipbuilding contracted radically and regained its all-male character. Most shipyard workers, even those who wanted to remain in their wartime trades, had to find jobs in other industries.[25]

All of these characteristics were particularly pronounced in the Portland-Vancouver area. Few experienced shipyard workers were available, since the three largest shipyards in the area were built during the war. The prewar population of both towns was so small that a severe labor shortage occurred early in the war, stimulating the early recruitment of women. For these reasons the Portland and Vancouver shipyards had the highest proportion of women production workers in the country. In the three Kaiser yards (which, because they were built during the war, had higher percentages of women than the older yards in the area), women composed 27 percent of the production work force in 1944, while they made up between about 10 and 20 percent of the production force in most other shipyard towns. Approximately 40,000 women were employed in the area's shipyards at the wartime employment peak. Because of the enormous demand for journeyman welders, the craft in which women were concentrated, an unusually high proportion of the women workers attained journeyman status at the Kaiser yards. In 1944 almost half the welding at one of the Kaiser shipyards was being done by women.[26]

At the end of the war, all three of the Kaiser yards and one of the smaller yards closed, leaving thousands of male and female workers looking for jobs in peacetime industries. The two small yards that continued to function retained only a small number of workers.[27]

An additional feature of the Portland and Vancouver area was the nationally acclaimed child-care program in each city. At the heart of the Portland program were the remarkable, innovative Kaiser Child Service Centers, two twenty-four–hour centers funded by the Maritime Commission and located at the shipyards. The history of child care in the Portland-Vancouver areas sheds some light on the confusing World War II child-care picture, one which was characterized by ambivalence on the part of government, industry, educators, and wage-earning mothers.[28]

In addition to government documents, archival collections, and periodicals, *Fleeting Opportunities* draws heavily on thirty-five interviews with women residents of the cities of Portland and Vancouver who worked in the shipyards during the war. The interviews were conducted in 1981 by me and the seven other members of the Northwest Women's History Project, and portions were used to produce the slide show "Good Work Sister! Women Shipyard Workers of World War II: An Oral History."[29] The narrators were selected from a pool of 200 women who responded to an article in a Portland daily newspaper. All 200 were interviewed on the phone and provided additional data for this study.

Using the suggestions of Sherna Gluck and Mary Rothchild, the Northwest Women's History Project attempted to select narrators who would reflect the composition of the female work force during the war in terms of age, race, marital status, and work experience as recorded by the Women's Bureau and local sources.[30] After reviewing our initial pool of volunteers we contacted various people and organizations to find additional black women and women who were in their late thirties and early forties during the war.[31] All the women we interviewed had worked in jobs that had been restricted to male workers before the war, since it was this experience that stimulated our interest in the project.[32] Approximately half of them had been journeymen.

These efforts were prompted by an interest in presenting a roughly representative variety of experiences, not as an effort to generate a scientifically correct sample. We recognized that our manner of contacting most of the narrators resulted in a group of women who felt that their experience in the wartime shipyards was significant and that this may not have been true for all women shipyard workers.

Oral history interviews present both problems and possibilities for understanding women's experience during and after World War II. There is, thanks to the assiduous efforts of the Women's Bureau staff, a wealth of statistical data and survey material. In addition, there is an emerging body of analysis of prescriptive literature both in popular culture and government propaganda. But aside from brief comments in Women's Bureau Bulletins and the accounts of women who were investigating defense work, we have few descriptions of the wartime and postwar experience by women workers themselves. Since so many of the unanswered questions about women, the war and reconversion are about consciousness, oral history interviews provide an invaluable additional source and can help to answer questions raised by the other material–particularly about women's attitudes. Because they present reflections about World War II and reconversion in the context of life histories, interviews are helpful in understanding the ways in which different elements interacted in the course of women's lives, and they add depth and texture to the analysis.

These oral histories are rich sources, not of an unmediated view of the past, but of recollections informed by what Ron Grele has called a "cultural vision" that shapes the way in which a narrator will seek order in the reconstruction of an event.[33] The cultural vision of each narrator emerges from the interaction of the individual's life experience and the values and attitudes that prevail in the environment in which she lives. In the forty years between the Second World War and the interviews I am using, there were three major shifts in the prevailing attitudes toward women and work. During the war women's work was celebrated and honored; war workers were, in Maureen Honey's words, the "heroines of the home front."[34] The cultural onslaught that occurred immediately after the war denigrated nondomestic female aspirations. During the 1970s, the rebirth of feminism spawned a reconsideration of women's relationship to work: a reaffirmation of women's right to meaningful work and an assault on discriminatory practices in the workplace. This shifting ideological context must have affected the way in which women recall and interpret their wartime and reconversion experiences. The oral history interview consists of events seen through the prism of subsequent experiences and influences. This phenomenon can, rather than invalidating the oral history material, enhance its value for illuminating changing consciousness.

As Ron Grele points out, oral history interviews are collective documents–"conversational narratives" in which both the interviewer and the narrator are active participants.[35] It is therefore important to note that the interviewers in this project approached the interviews with questions that arose from the feminist reevaluation of women and work. We represented the third layer of cultural interpretation described above. Although we tried to create an atmosphere in which the narrator felt free to express herself and did not feel pressured to adhere to particular beliefs, it is probable that our questions, as well as the less controllable aspects of our behavior, affected the interviews. This, too, need not be seen as invalidating the material, but as generating dialogue between the past and the present.

For example, Ruth Drurey, one of the shipyard workers in this study, says in her interview:

> Thinking back on it, it is odd that some of us didn't band together and try to stay in the metal trades, particularly those of us who were good at it. But we didn't; we just accepted what was handed to us and didn't think anything about it.[36]

This reflection emerged from the interaction of three factors: my question, the contemporary cultural context and Drurey's experience in the postwar years. My question, "Did the general attitude toward women change after the war?" focused Drurey's attention on changing norms for women's behavior. In her experience as a lone woman supervisor in a government agency, she had successfully challenged the expectations of male authority. This enabled her to look back at the postwar period with an awareness of the possibilities for intervention. Lastly, I suspect that Drurey might not have made this observation if the interview had taken place in 1959 before the resurgence of feminism.

If, as Jesse Lemisch suggests, memory is an active process of construction in which the search for order and meaning renders some images clearer than others, we face specific problems when we try to reconstruct unrealized expectations or feelings of anger or disappointment.[37] Because there was no political movement in the 1940s to validate any feelings of anger that women workers may have felt after their exclusion from their wartime trades, such feelings may have been transmuted into more adaptive attitudes.[38]

Interpreted with these considerations in mind, the thirty-five oral history interviews with former shipyard workers contain a wealth of material about women's perspectives on their wartime and postwar experiences that will be used in conjunction with other sources. By illuminating the points at which women took initiative, the interviews enable us to see women as actors and they generate information about issues such as sexual harassment that elude the written record.

Fleeting Opportunities is organized into five chapters. It begins by describing the process by which industry and government recruited women to shipyard jobs and then moves to a discussion of the women who were attracted to shipyard work. In contrast to the prevailing notion that the women shipyard workers were emerging en masse from their kitchens, chapter 1 sketches a variety of pre war experiences, seeking to connect women's wartime work with their lives before the war. Chapter 2 describes the shipyard world as women experienced it. The yards provided women with opportunities and challenges but reinforced their transient and alien status in a variety of ways: the enduring divisions between men's and women's work, the racial and sexual hierarchy of the yards, the preoccupation with female sexuality, the actual and threatened sexual harassment.

The domestic responsibilities of women wage earners posed problems for an industry that depended on their labor. Chapter 3 examines the responses of government, industry, and the community to "the double day." It focuses particularly on the history of the child-care programs in the Portland-Vancouver area, a history that demonstrates the community's ambivalence about wage earning mothers. Chapter 3 also describes in some detail the achievements of the Kaiser Child Service Centers.

In chapters 4 and 5 the focus widens to include a brief overview of the national picture in order to provide a context for the local material. Beginning with a brief survey of attitudes throughout the country, chapter 4 examines wartime attitudes toward the postwar future of women wage earners, demonstrating that despite the mixed messages of the shipyard world, more than half of the women production workers in the Portland-Vancouver shipyards nurtured hopes of continuing to use their wartime-acquired skills in the peacetime world.

Chapter 5 is divided into two sections. The bulk of the chapter examines the reconversion period during which women were excluded from skilled industrial work by unions and industry. While there were some efforts on a national level to protect the rights of women in the reconversion period, women shipyard workers in the Portland-Vancouver area who wanted to continue using their new skills had no organizational support, and most found jobs in low-paid, predominantly female occupations. Chapter 5 concludes with a sketch of the contours of the female work force in 1950 and demonstrates that while women continued to enter and reenter the job market throughout the 1950s and 1960s, a narrow range of choices shaped their lives. The women who did challenge the limitations they encountered did so in isolation, but their stories suggest that beneath the quiescence of the postwar world lay hidden pockets of female defiance.

1 ☆ "WORKING WOMEN WIN WARS"

The Shipbuilding Boom
in Portland and Vancouver

In 1940 the Portland-Vancouver area was a commercial center for the surrounding lumber and ranching area. Of the 318,788 people living in the two towns only one-sixth (53,131) were industrially employed.[1] To a great extent, it was the actions of Henry Kaiser and his son Edgar that were responsible for the creation of the war boom that transformed the life of the two cities. Henry Kaiser, described by one contemporary as a "rolling mountain of a man just full of ideas," had been involved in a variety of building projects.[2] His reputation as the "fabulous Kaiser" resulted from the construction of the San Francisco Bay Bridge and the Grand Coulee, Hoover and Bonneville Dams. Edgar Kaiser was one of six young men working with Henry Kaiser and had been the general manager of the Grand Coulee Dam. The Kaisers were new to shipbuilding, but by the end of the war they had built seven shipyards on the Pacific Coast, acquired interests in seven others, and played a central role in shaping the wartime shipbuilding program, which brought them enormous profits.[3]

Between January 1941 and March 1942, the Kaiser Corporation built two large shipyards in Portland and one in Vancouver and negotiated lucrative contracts with the U.S. Maritime Commission. Three smaller shipyards – Willamette Iron and Steel (WISCO), Commerical Iron Works, and Albina Engine and Machine Works – had been in operation before the war and were also awarded government contracts.[4] By December 1, 1942, the six shipyards in the Portland area employed 92,273 men and women and the city had become a shipyard boom town.[5]

Changes in the shipbuilding process allowed the wartime shipyards to produce ships with unprecedented speed. The use of welding rather than riveting to assemble the ships saved labor, time, and repair costs. Welded ships were put together in large subassemblies, which allowed much of the work to be done in fabricating shops at the shipyards.[6] The subassemblies (such as bottoms, deck, bulkheads) were then welded together on the ways (the structures on which the ship is built and launched).[7] As Deborah Hirschfield has shown, these changes allowed the shipyards to hire workers who were specifically trained as welders rather than skilled craftsmen. With the cooperation of the shipbuilding unions, the lengthy apprenticeship system by which a worker had become a journeyman was replaced by training for specific skills. While the term journeyman was retained, it no longer carried its prewar meaning, which implied the mastery of several different skills.[8] As a result the shipyards were able to hire thousands of unskilled workers and train them quickly to become journeymen welders. While the shipyard unions had agreed to change the training system, there was some distress among workers at Oregon Ship that workers who were new to shipbuilding were put to work as welders and "rapidly advanced to leaders" while the "older men are forced to work under kids whom they have taught the little they know."[9]

The local labor supply quickly became inadequate for the needs of the shipyards and was further depleted by the increasing numbers of men who were drafted in late 1942 and early 1943. Some of the Portland-Vancouver plants involved in war production threatened to shut down if more labor did not become available, and some of the shipyard managements began to actively recruit workers outside the Pacific Northwest.[10]

The Kaiser shipyards sent recruiters all over the country and chartered trains to transport workers. Workers poured into the area.[11] By 1942, 120,000 people were working in Portland's war plants and more were needed. The swollen population strained the area's resources, causing the most acute housing shortage in the country. Vanport, the largest war housing project in the world, was under construction but would not be completed until September 1943.[12] Organized labor criticized Kaiser's continued recruitment of workers in the face of the housing shortage. Overcrowded schools and inadequate public transportation increased the tension in the community, and pressure mounted on the shipbuilding industry to hire people who had already migrated to the area but were not employed.[13]

Can Women Build Ships?

Because prewar shipbuilding was an almost entirely male industry, neither management nor government considered hiring women to work in the shipyards until there was no other alternative.[14] Throughout 1941 and early 1942 articles in local newspapers speculating about the possible recruitment of women for war work were often written in a sarcastic and incredulous vein and frequently presented the female production worker as an improbable and ridiculous notion. Bonnie Wiley, for example, a staff writer for *The Oregonian*, began a series in the fall of 1941 in which she described her visits to various industrial sites in a self-consciously feminine style. "Electricity to me has always been something that happened when I turned on the switch. I'd much rather leave it at that. If war comes I think I'll stick to reporting."[15] *The Bo's'n's Whistle*, the house organ of the Kaiser shipyards, was also dubious. In March, 1942, it published a full-page cartoon, depicting what might happen if women were hired in the plate shop. It featured women in high heels teetering precariously over heavy machinery and performing a variety of inappropriate, inept and "feminine" acts.[16]

Despite such skepticism, the recruitment and training of women shipbuilders was underway by early 1942. In February the City of Portland and the War Manpower Commission organized a house-to-house survey to assess the availability of female labor and asked Saidie Dunbar, former president of General Federation of Women's Clubs and member of the Women's Advisory Committee of the War Manpower Commission to direct it.[17] In April the first women were enrolled in the state-run welding training program.[18]

Federally funded state-run training operated at Benson High School in Portland from 3:30 p.m. to 9:30 p.m. each day, and, by July 1942, 14 percent of its students were women.[19] Women were also being trained at private welding schools such as one run by Mr. and Mrs. McPherson, who trained ten women welders in the basement of their home in May, 1942.[20] Training to be a journeyman welder involved learning to weld in three different positions – flat, vertical and horizontal – and took from ten days to four weeks. Some welding courses also included overhead welding, which was more difficult and was not included in the standard test that students took at the completion of training.[21] As the labor shortage intensified, workers were sometimes hired at the shipyards as soon as they had learned how to tack weld, the most basic welding skill.[22]

In April 1942, the first two women welders were hired by the Kaiser Corporation. Most women were hired as helpers at first, but as the demand for journeyman welders increased, so did the number of women welders. As the female production worker became a reality, people began to challenge the assumption, expressed in the *Bo's'n's Whistle* cartoon, that women were unsuited for heavy industrial work. In May 1942, for example, William Witherow of the National Association of Manufacturers, assured representatives of 500 com-

Bo's'n's Whistle, March 26, 1942.   *Courtesy of the Oregon Historical Society.*

panies that "there is little difference between men and women as regards their satisfactory performance in industry."[23]

Women and the Unions

Women had been working in shipyard production jobs for several months before they were admitted to the major shipyard unions. In May 1941, a week before ship construction began, Oregon Shipbuilding Corporation, the first yard built by Kaiser in the area, signed a closed shop agreement with the AFL Metal Trades Council.[24] As soon as the other yards were built, they entered into similar agreements with the Metal Trades council. Since thousands of workers were subsequently hired by the shipyards, and only sixty-six people were working in the shipyards when the contract was signed, the CIO's Industrial Union of Marine and Shipbuilding Workers of America (IUMSWA) filed charges with the National Labor Relations Board in November 1941, claiming that the majority of workers did not elect the AFL Metal Trades Unions as their bargaining agent. The National Labor Relations Board decided favorably on the IUMSWA grievance and filed a complaint against the Kaiser yards. The case dragged on throughout the war until it was rendered moot by an amendment to an appropriations bill passed by Congress in June, 1943 that barred the National Labor Relations Board from considering complaints about labor agreements that were over three months old.[25]

The International Brotherhood of Boilermakers, Iron Shipbuilders, Blacksmiths, Forgers and Helpers (the Boilermakers), one of the metal trades unions, controlled two thirds of the industrial jobs in the shipyard. The Boilermakers Union, which had never admitted women members, was suddenly confronted by an influx of women workers into industrial trades in shipyards all over the country. In July 1942, after a group of women welders demonstrated at the headquarters of the San Francisco Local, the Boilermakers International submitted a resolution to its membership to amend the constitution to "remove the restriction on female membership and permit acceptance of their applications."[26] The resolution was framed as a wartime measure, asserting that the union was compelled to "depart from many long established practices" since it was in "honor and duty bound to support the war effort." Since the war crisis had necessitated the introduction of female labor in the shipbuilding industry and the union shop agreement required all workers to belong to the Boilermakers, many locals had appealed for a change.[27]

In Local 72, the Portland branch of the Boilermakers' union, the resolution sparked controversy. The day before members were to vote on the question, the editor of the local Boilermakers newspaper, *The Shipbuilder*, commented, "There's going to be a 'Hot Time in the Old Town' this weekend when members of Local 72 traipse down to the Boilermakers building to cast their votes on a 'yes' or 'no' decision as to whether women are to be allowed equal membership to their union." A letter in the same issue of *The Shipbuilder* suggests that this issue was very much on the minds of the male workers who were being asked to vote on the measure. The author of the letter, Marion Easterly, commented that "the boys who think it's O.K. to let women into the Boilermakers aren't going to vote," while those "who don't want competition from us gals are going to stomp righteously down to the Boilermakers Building on Saturday August 22 ESPECIALLY to vote NO! Those boys seem mostly to figure like this: 'Gosh if we let women into the union now, they'll take our jobs away from us after war.'"[28]

Easterly's response is interesting because of both what she said and what she omitted. She did not argue that women had a right to belong to the union and should have equal opportunity to enter skilled industrial work. But she also avoided promises that would support the expectation that women would happily leave the industrial work force after the war. She argued instead that those who opposed the admission of women to the union were obstructing the war effort, and if women were not admitted to the union they would work as nonunion workers. Lastly she warned, "If you are afraid of a large UNION supply of skilled labor after the war just WHAT do you think a large NON UNION supply is going to do to your jobs? Give us a break," Easterly concluded. "WE'D RATHER BE SISTERS THAN SCABS!"[29]

Evidently most members of the International Brotherhood did not, in Easterly's words, "bother to vote." While most of the locals that participated in the election approved the resolution, the number of votes cast fell below the number required to change the union's constitution. Many factors may have contributed to the low level of participation in the International election, but it is clear that there was no great enthusiasm for admitting women to union membership even as an emergency measure.[30] The Executive Council decided to take action on its own, and in September the International president directed the "gentlemen and brothers" of the member locals to admit women. Women's applications were to be sent to the International headquarters, where they would be kept segregated, and locals were instructed to "be sure to mark on the margin . . . FEMALE."[31] The issue of the *Shipbuilder* that followed the referendum was silent on the results of the vote, but its regular Swan Island column reported, "For the first time in history we have ladies for boilermakers' helpers hired and put on the job by the Boilermakers union and they are doing a good job too."[32]

A final obstacle to the integration of women into the shipyard work-force was the state legislation, which since the beginning of the twentieth century had reinforced the exclusion of women from skilled industrial work by regulating their wages and working conditions. The Oregon law prohibiting women from lifting over twenty-five pounds and carrying over fifteen pounds came under particular fire from war industries, and in October 1942 the Wages and Hours Commission agreed to grant waivers to plants demonstrating that compliance with the restrictions would impede the war effort.[33]

Recruiting Women

Access to the major shipbuilding union and modification of restrictive legislation facilitated the recruitment of women for war work, and during the last few months of 1942 women joined the shipyard work force in increasing numbers. By the end of the year 17 percent of the shipyard workers at Kaiser, Vancouver, and 11 percent at Oregon Ship and Swan Island were women. While Oregon Shipbuilding was the first shipyard in the country to hire women to work in the yards, it employed a smaller percentage of women workers because it had been built earlier and had recruited much of its labor force before the shortage of male labor became acute.[34]

The three non-Kaiser shipyards in the area, Willamette Iron and Steel (WISCO), Commercial Iron Works, and Albina Engine and Machine Works, expanded rapidly during 1942 and 1943, and as the labor shortage intensified, their managements overcame whatever resistance they had to recruiting women industrial workers. The management of Commercial Iron Works, for example, had explicitly opposed hiring women throughout 1942, but by March 1943 its position had softened, and five hundred women were doing production work (5 percent of the work force).[35]

The first women industrial workers at the shipyard entered either as helpers in various crafts for which they needed little or no training or as welders, which the shipyard needed desperately. At the end of 1942 and the beginning of 1943, increasing numbers of women began entering shipyard crafts other than welding. The International Brotherhood of Electrical Workers (IBEW) admitted women workers but enforced a rigid hierarchy in which journeyman status was granted to only 5 percent of all workers. The IBEW also refused admission to women under eighteen and over thirty-five.[36] At first women electricians were confined to the shops, but in the fall of 1942 *The Oregonian* announced that "it has been discovered that women can replace many men on jobs in ship wiring."[37] In February 1943 the Machinists union agreed to train women and to accept them as members after one hundred hours of training. By April, two hundred women machinists were being sought by local shipbuilding companies.[38]

Government and industry presented their campaign to recruit women to work in the shipyards as an effort to convince non-wage-earning women that "working women win wars," and claimed that their training programs made "welders out of housewives."[39] The history of the mobilization, however, tells a somewhat different story. The most dramatic growth in the female labor force in the shipyards took place during the first half of 1943, when women comprised 65 percent of the new workers in the shipyards.[40] Early in 1943 the management of most retail stores had agreed, at the urging of the War Manpower Commission, to facilitate the transfer of their workers to war industries. Most of these workers were female, since in 1940 half of the clerks in Portland stores were women, and by 1943 the proportion was substantially higher as a result of the draft.[41] In February workers were being shifted from nonessential industries to war production at the rate of one thousand a week.[42] It is clear that a substantial number of the female shipyard workers were coming not from their kitchens but from the female-dominated segment of the work force.

In contrast, the mobilization efforts of the spring and summer, which were clearly directed at housewives, were less productive. In May 1943 Sara Southall and Thelma McKelvey, who had been sent by the War Manpower Commission to investigate the utilization of women in the three Kaiser Shipyards, commended the Kaiser yards on their employment of women but suggested that more women could be effectively used. They urged the local War Manpower commission to "immediately make plans for an intensive recruiting drive for women in the Portland area."[43]

At the end of May, radios and newspapers were filled with advertisements for women shipyard workers. "It was just times," remembered LueRayne Culbertson, "when everybody went to the shipyards. 'We need you!'—and it was on every station, you turn the radio on; it was 'we need you!' "[44] But the Kaiser management reported that the three-week radio and newspaper drive had not recruited any additional women welders. Edgar Kaiser, perhaps in an effort to justify continued recruitment from outside the area, concluded in a letter to Admiral Vikery that the lack of response to the media campaign was "a definite indication that the Portland area now has an acute shortage of women available for war work as well as men."[45] Nevertheless, government and industry intensified their efforts to mobilize local women. In June 1943, the United States Employment Service (USES), the War Manpower Commission and local women's organizations joined forces to organize a "Working Women Win Wars Week." Organizers distinguished the campaign from the earlier surveys of women workers by describing it as a "definite effort to recruit for some kind of war work or service, every woman in Multnomah County who is eligible for full or part time employment."[46] At the kickoff rally, J. N. Riley, the naval shipbuilding supervisor, announced that local plants planned to move toward a shipyard work force that was one-third women. Women, he asserted, were "not only the equal of men in working efficiency, but in manifold cases they are superior to men in turning out the weapons of war."[47]

While publicity described the campaign as an effort to recruit all women, it was clearly directed at housewives. The neighborhood was the basic unit of the campaign, block leaders canvassed women during the day, and daytime demonstrations of industrial skills were held in local department stores. Berenice Thompson, who hired on as a welder at Commercial Iron Works in 1943, recalls the neighborhood canvassers "asking all the ladies: 'I don't care if you have an education c.' not, we'll find a job for you.'"[49] While the rate of increase in the female labor force never equalled that of the first half of 1943, the number of women employed at the Vancouver and Portland shipyards did continue to grow through 1943 and 1944, and by the spring of 1944, women composed 27 percent of the shipyard work force in the Kaiser yards.[49]

Who Were the Women War Workers?

The experience of most of the women who "flocked to war work" did not conform to the image of "housewife turned welder" that dominated the recruitment campaigns, an image whose tenacity has contributed to the distortion of the history of women wage earners during and after the war. The Moses Plan, for example, a proposal for a postwar public works project, began its narrative with an assessment of the employment needs of Portland's population that assumed that most of the women workers would "retire from the work force" to "resume houshold duties."[50] This assumption belied the realities of many women's lives in two ways. Over half of the women who worked in the shipyards had been in the work force before the war, and many of those who had not been employed were discouraged workers who were unable to find jobs during the depression.[51]

Women's varied responses to surveys about their prewar occupations illustrate the complexity of the prewar experience of women war workers. In a survey of 90 percent of the workers at the three Kaiser yards in the Portland-Vancouver area, respondents were asked to report their prewar occupations and were offered the following choices: farmer, housewife, white collar, laborer, skilled labor, professional or proprietor, service, other, or no previous occupation and no response. Forty-one percent of the 21,619 women who responded to this survey described themselves as housewives.[52] In contrast, only 20 percent of the respondents reported that they were engaged in home housework when asked, "What were you doing the week before Pearl Harbor?" in a Woman's Bureau Survey of 30,000 households in different parts of the country.[53] In the Kaiser survey there was no category for unemployed or students, and women who had been unemployed may have described themselves as housewives. Thus the inaccuracy of the term housewife may account for the disparity between the results of the two surveys.[54]

Women who described themselves as housewives may have been employed before the war but saw their work as temporary or secondary to their family roles. This did not mean, however, that they did not work for wages or were unavailable or uninterested in waged work. Alice Kessler-Harris has pointed out that the number of women in the work force had been increasing steadily since 1900 – at an average of 6 percent per decade – and suggests that the depression created a backlog of discouraged workers. The number of women who joined the work force during the war years, she argues, "reflects continuity with previous attempts by some women to break out of traditional roles."[55] In the period after World War II, Kessler-Harris suggests, an increasing number of women began to see the possibility of combining waged and household work.[56]

The testimony of the women narrators supports this interpretation and reveals women attempting to combine household and waged work before, during, and after the war. The narrators did not see work inside and outside the home as incompatible, and whether or not women were employed depended to a great extent on whether jobs were available. The following examples of women's work lives before the war illuminate the factors that affected their choices about work and family and the interplay between consciousness and experience that surveys obscure. Their stories suggest that behind the category "housewife" may lie the discouraged worker who stopped looking for work because there was little available during the Depression, the seasonal worker (particularly women who worked in canneries and on fruit farms) who may not have seen this as permanent employment, and various forms of "invisible" work such as taking in laundry, caring for children, and selling eggs.

Sixteen of the thirty-six narrators were employed before the war. Half of these women were married, and the rest were divorced or single. Half of the employed women had children, including several of the single and divorced women. The eight married wage earners illustrate a trend indicated by national and local statistics. Despite the general sentiment against married women working outside the home during the Depression (George Gallup reported that he had "never seen respondents so solidly united in opposition on any subject imaginable including sin and hay fever"), the percentage of wage-earning women who were married rose from 29 to 35 percent between 1930 and 1940.[57] Like most wage-earning women, the narrators worked in low-paid, traditionally female fields: domestic, clerical, factory, and restaurant work and child care. All of them described themselves as needing to work whether they were married, single, or divorced but remembered vividly the difficulty of finding work that would adequately support them.

Few had any formal training. "And of course," commented Etta Harvey, who had married when she was eighteen and had a child a year later, "I hadn't really taken any education that would have prepared me for the working world so I had to take menial labor and I went to work as a waitress."[58] Marie Merchant, like most black wage-earning women, worked as a domestic before coming from Kentucky to Oregon to work in the shipyards. Her weekly wage of $3.00 was typical of what Jacqueline Jones has described as the "radically depressed wages" of domestic work during the Depression.[59]

Three of the narrators who were working before the war had some occupational training. Two were part of the growing number of women who were preparing themselves for secretarial work. The third had trained in a traditionally male field, landscape architecture, but finding the field closed to women had been working in the advertising department of a woolen mill.[60]

The stories of the narrators who described themselves as housewives before the war reveal two hidden phenomena that expand the meaning of the term housewife. Several of them had recently experienced a change in their family situation that made it necessary for them to support themselves and their children, and several were earning money doing the "invisible" work that historians and sociologists are recognizing played an important role in family life throughout the nineteenth and the first half of the twentieth centuries.[61]

Four of the self-described "housewives" found themselves faced with the need to work for wages when the war broke out, but in only one case was this a result of the war. Like several of the women who had already found jobs before the war, they were not attached to breadwinning men and therefore needed to support themselves. Alice Erickson's husband had died, and she was determined not to become dependent on her children. Fortunately, at the point at which Erickson needed to enter the work force, shipyard work became available to women. "I needed to work," she commented, "and that was the best-paying work that I could get so naturally I took it."[62] Audrey Moore's husband had left her with a small child when she was seventeen, so she went to work in a lumber mill in Louisiana that was hiring women as a result of the wartime labor shortage.[63] Pat Rowland's marriage was breaking up, and to support herself and her children she hired on at the shipyards.[64] Nell Conley, like many other servicemen's wives, did not receive her husband's allotment from the Navy for three months after he left, and she found it insufficient when it came. She got a job at Meier and Frank, a local department store, but she found the pay inadequate to support herself and her child.[65] Three of these four women, while they had not been employed before the war, would have been looking for paid work even if there had not been a war.

Several of the married women with husbands at home would also have been working for wages if jobs had been available. Ree Adkins had been a teacher before she quit to have children. She wanted to return to teaching but found herself a victim of the widespread discrimination against married women teachers during the Depression. In 1941 only 13 percent of school districts in the United States would hire married women. Adkins's perception was that she "couldn't go back to teaching. It was only for men's jobs.[66]

Nona Pool, Billie Strmiska, and Beatrice Hadley all had difficulty finding work but found ways to make money in various forms of "invisible work," an essential ingredient of what Jeanne Westin has called "making do" during the Depression.[67] Like thousands of other people during the Depression, Nona Pool, Billie Strmiska, and their husbands traveled in search of work.[68] The Pools lived primarily in lumber camps. "Course there was no work for women," commented Pool;

during the winter months I'd like to make a little extra money – I always was looking for work but never could find any. . . . But the tie hacks [railroad tie workers] always wanted to go downtown and get themselves boozed up on the weekends so I got to washing shirts. I'd wash and iron shirts with those little sad irons, chop the wood to keep the fire going, hauling water to do the laundry and get twenty-five cents a shirt. . . . I made pretty good money doing the shirts. When I got everything organized, why I could do eight to ten shirts.[69]

Billie Strmiska also had difficulty finding full-time work so she and her husband traveled around picking berries and canning vegetables, fruit, and fish before she went to work at the shipyard.[70]

Beatrice Hadley said of the Depression, "You couldn't buy a job. You couldn't even steal one." Hadley's prewar life is a searing illustration of the profound costs of the economic oppression of women. She had been working for a living since she was ten. "I raised myself," she commented, and "I raised myself to work." When she was sixteen she worked as a chambermaid in a hotel in a small town in Iowa. One of the regular guests, a man twice her age, proposed marriage, promising that once married she "wouldn't have to work those long hours." She married and had three children. After years of physical abuse she left her husband, leaving her three children behind since she knew she couldn't support them. Hadley remarried and worked at various jobs throughout the twenties and early thirties. She and her second husband moved to Oregon in 1926 and worked in a pickle factory for eight years. Their response to the unemployment of the Depression was to move to Washington, where they bought a small piece of land and raised chickens and calves, which they bought young and fed with goat's milk. Their farm was very much a joint venture, and Hadley always thought of herself as a worker.[71]

While some people moved back to the land during the Depression, others were driven off it by the plummeting prices of farm products. Helen Berggren and her husband were running a dairy farm in Washington; unable to make enough money to support their five children, they both went to work in the shipyards. The year before they moved to Vancouver lives in Berggren's memory as one of extreme poverty. "We had so little money," she remembers,

and no relief, no Red Cross, nothing. And nothing grew because it was so late; frost came so early then. So we ate little potatoes but then we got wheat from somewhere and had that taken to the mill

Billie Strmiska, one of the narrators and winner of a welding contest. *Courtesy of the Oregon Historical Society, negative #62064.*

and got some flour. So I didn't eat but I drank the milk from the cows and many a night and many a day I only drank milk.[72]

Rosa Dickson and her husband were raising cotton in Texas when the "bottom fell out of the price of cotton. We left our farm," she recalls. "We couldn't make expenses, the cotton lay in the fields." The Dicksons traveled to Arizona, where Mr. Dickson worked in the copper mines. Although the war had begun to create labor shortages, the mines did not hire women, so Rosa bought a part interest in a self-service laundry. They then heard about the shipyards in Oregon and drove out West.[73]

None of these women's prewar lives conformed to the image of the housewife summoned by patriotic duty to leave a home in which she had been exclusively engaged in domestic work. While they were glad to participate in the war effort, most of the narrators were looking for ways to earn money whether they were married or not.

Many women thought of themselves as "workers" – a term which to them included a variety of activities: unpaid domestic work, work on the family farm, part-time and seasonal work such as picking fruit, self-employment such as washing shirts, as well as full-time waged labor.[74] Their various forms of work were inextricably woven together in efforts to support themselves and contribute to the family resources, efforts which were constrained by the limited opportunities available to women and the prevailing expectation that women would not need vocational education or training.

The reflections of the narrators about the ways their socialization had limited them and left them without marketable skills illuminates the complex interaction between women's choices and constraints they faced in their lives. Nona Pool grew up on a farm in Nebraska, and her father made her quit school "because he said it cost too much for a girl to go to school because they just go get married anyway. I was waiting to get married till I finished school," she recalled, but "when my dad said quit school I decided I'd get married then. I was tired of that farm life."[75] Lois Housman remembers that in her childhood,

I always wanted to be an engineer. That was the height of my ambition . . . and then I thought wireless telegraphy was just as close to that as I could get. And then I had a friend there in Rogersville and he was the depot agent, and I used to go down and listen to him and he'd tell me what these little clicks meant, you know. It was fascinating. . . . I wanted to learn wireless telegraphy and my dad he didn't think that girls ought to be out like that – just was no place for a girl. And he thought cooking was my gait. He said that if you knew how to cook why that was all – just keep house and cook. So I didn't get to go. . . . I could've went to Springfield and learnt but he didn't want me to.[76]

For these women and thousands like them, the recruitment of women for shipyard work meant an end to years of frustrated attempts to find satisfying work that paid decently.

Joining Up

While joining the shipyard workforce was applauded by government, media and industry as a glorious act of patriotism, it remained a difficult thing for women to do. Women were very conscious of penetrating a male bastion and sometimes sought the support of friends and relatives as they went through the hiring and training process. "With two of us together," commented Pat Koehler, "we had enough nerve to sign up as electricians."[77] Shipyard work was, like any new field of activity for women, surrounded by rumors and prejudices. "Mom wished I wouldn't," said Virginia Larson, "because it wasn't where nice girls worked." Her parents had heard the shipyard was a "terrible tough place."[78] Rosa Dickson's husband, who got a job in the shipyards himself, shared their concern. While he supported his wife's decision to look for work, he objected to her proposal that she work in the shipyards.

> He said, "Oh, you cannot work down there in the shipyards. They're too rough and the language is bad," and all of these kind of things which I was not used to. I tried Ward's. I tried lots of other places. You know what they paid? Seventy-six cents an hour. That was about the average base pay Meier and Frank's, anybody, had at that time. And I said, well I'm not gonna take a job like that because the shipyards are paying the big money. . . . I says I been on the busses. You can't tell me a thing about the people. I know the winos on there, I know the swearing on there and it cannot be any worse down there.[79]

Women's motives for joining the shipyard workforce were varied. Some, like Doris Avshalomov, saw patriotism as primary in their decisions to become shipyard workers. Avshalomov was in college during the early part of World War II, and many of her friends were drafted. When she graduated she found it difficult to have "strong personal ambitions" with the world in such crisis.

> It was just a very weighty thing to be living in; almost as if the world wasn't real any more. It wasn't as if you could think about yourself. You were thinking about what a terrible state the world was in. . . . It was kind of a patriotic decision because I have a very strong bias against anything military and yet I felt that with the war on and with

everyone I knew involved in it, it would be appropriate for me to be involved too.[80]

While most of the narrators needed to work and were attracted to the high wages of shipbuilding, being able to help the war effort was also important to them; it added meaning to their work. Nell Conley, who went to the shipyards with a good friend, explained their reasons for doing so: "We both had to work, we both had children, so we became welders, and if I might say so, damn good ones." When asked what was the most important thing for us to understand about women shipyards workers, however, Conley commented, "In spite of the fact that shipyard work paid better, that was the last of our concern; we felt we were doing something for the country."[81] For some women, however, patriotism was eclipsed by pressing economic need. "There's no use in saying I did it for patriotism," commented Kathryn Blair. "It was pure economics. It was the one thing where I could make enough money to get along."[82]

Shipbuilding was one of the highest paying industries in the country, and the money was a major motive for most of the narrators.[83] To women, whose earnings ranged from $20 a month plus room and board to $70 for office work, the shipyard wages, averaging $230 a month for skilled workers, were dazzling. Even Betty Cleator, who had a relatively well-paid office job, was astonished by the shipyard wages. "It was an unbelievable amount of money, just unbelievable. I'm not sure but what I was making more than my father, and he was a professional forester – had been with the forest service all those years."[84] "The money was too good to pass up," commented Jean Clark, who quit high school in order to work in the shipyards.[85]

The high shipyard wages figured in women's lives in a variety of ways, and often represented not only an economic improvement but a symbol of capability. Economic independence and self-respect are closely intertwined in women's recollection of their decision to work in the shipyards. "I had an object in mind," recalled Etta Harvey. "I had a son to raise and I also wanted to prove that women were reliable and capable. I mean, it was something I had to prove to myself and to whoever I could get the message to."[86] Berenice Thompson was married and had grown children when she joined up at the shipyards against her husband's wishes. "I had been very poor and worked very hard and it meant a lot to me, for that money, and besides it meant a lot just to prove myself. My husband was from Kentucky. He didn't think women knew anything. So I showed him." Mr. Thompson was not converted immediately. He resisted for some time before moving into the house that his wife had bought with her shipyard wages.[87]

For women who had been working at other jobs, the appeal of the shipyard was often a combination of high wages and the promise of more interesting and rewarding work. The money was a definite advantage, according to Loena Ellis, "and it was an opportunity that was too good to miss. As far as the work went it was terrific because, gee, I was treated like a human being, you know, instead of part of the machinery." Ellis had been working at a burlap bag factory and found shipyard work a great deal more exciting.

> Oh, I tell you it was being let out of a cage! The job I worked on before was anchored to one spot all day long, running a machine breathing burlap, steady noise, we learned to read lips, and we only escaped through our imagination. It was so routine that you did it without thinking and so your thoughts were elsewhere. And the shipyard was all activity, moving about and different things.[88]

Graveyard Shift, Vancouver Ship

Doris Avshalomov

Graveyard shift, moths going aboard in the summer night,
our crew looked for each other between shadows
and met in half-dark of caged bulbs.
We could side-step the meaning then.

Each hull came off the ways named for a battle –
Kwajalein, Leyte, Iwo Jima. Crews on Outfitting
dressed their parts: electricians bristling with tools,
painters smeared white against the spray,
scalers weighed heavy with grime,
welders – necromancers in leather hood and gloves.

A welder works alone. No one may look without a mask.
Striking the arc with a sting, he melts the rod in
with an even hiss. Through the dark mask as from a cave
you watch the blinding arc move slowly into its crack.
My arm, too quick, froze the rod to the deck, stubbed it out.

Nights without chippers we could listen for the high ring
of crane operators, lords of the outfitting dock.
Swinging supplies out of the air, they whistled to us
from their eyries, invited us up. Should I go?
I ask a rigger, yearning towards the high bright cage.
But there were rules.

Nights when chippers were leveling welds the hull
became a giant bell, ringing with the thrust of power chisels.
Their arms and shoulders bulged. They never spoke,
swathed in their clangor. Near them, our soles
tingled through our boots. Ears rang for days.

By winter we could feel a change.
Rain pressed down from no sky, pinned us against the dock,
river invisible. We saw each other as wraiths,
coming at midnight, disappearing at dawn, bruised
by cold metal and incessant din. Even from the flight deck
there was no sunrise for us.

2 ☆ LIFE IN THE YARDS

"Women in ordinary times do not belong in shipyards any more than men belong in foxholes," one shipyard newspaper reminded its readers in 1943.[1] Women shipyard workers, like schrapnel and torpedoes, were an unfortunate necessity to be tolerated with grim good humor. This outlook permeated the workplace and the community throughout the war, assuaging fears that the female invasion of male turf would permanently subvert the sexual division of labor.

In Portland and Vancouver, as in the rest of the country, the recruitment of women for shipyard work occurred only when the demand for labor made it unavoidable.[2] Each new barrier was crossed with reluctance and elaborately justified in terms of contemporary notions of femininity as well as wartime exigencies. This spirit did not fade as the proportion of women production workers grew to surpass all other U.S. shipyards. As in defense industries throughout the country, the re-creation of the sexual division of labor, the persistence of sex discrimination, and the pervasive emphasis on female sexuality combined to reinforce the sexual order.

But while the resilience of sexism manifested itself in myriad ways, it did not entirely define the experience of the women who took industrial jobs in the shipyards. While the new opportunities were surrounded by constraints and limitations, they did represent an unprecedented opening in what had previously been an impenetrable barrier. At times women adjusted to the constraints and limitations they found, at times they were defeated by them and left their shipyard jobs, but at times, finding the doors open a crack and strengthened by the sense of capability they developed in the shipyards, women pushed the doors open even further and shaped their shipyard experience to meet their needs.

What Can Women Do?

In its three-volume 1943 study of the Kaiser shipyards, the Oregon division of the War Manpower Commission devoted substantial attention to the women workers "whose employment presented many complicated problems."[3] While problems may have been complicated, they were only partially attributable to the women themselves. Dorothy Newman, in her report on the Women's Bureau survey of thirty-five shipyards, commented that "problems that are brought to the attention of those interested in women's success often stem as much from attitudes towards women workers in the man's world of shipbuilding as from the actual situation."[4] While most women's lack of familiarity with skilled industrial work did require some additional training, and their responsibility for domestic work created a need for new services, a host of other problems were generated, not by the women workers but by the threat their presence posed to cultural beliefs and patriarchal institutions.

The reproduction of sex segregation in the shipyards helped to diffuse this threat. Someone entering the yards who was shocked by the unfamiliar sight of women production workers could be reassured by the familiar sight of women clustered in certain jobs. While the barriers that excluded women from production work had been lowered, they reappeared in the shipyards as divisions between men's and women's work. The majority of women production workers were helpers or semiskilled workers; the only craft in which a large number of women achieved journeyman status was welding. (See Table 1 for a comparison of the occupational breakdown of male and female workers at Swan Island.) In her astute analysis of sex segregation in the Kaiser yards, Karen Beck Skold calculated an index of sex segregation indicating that 50 percent of the workers would have had to change jobs in order to equally distribute female and male workers in the shipyard production force.[5]

Images of a sex-segregated world dominate the memories of the narrators. Women production workers in the shipyard, according to Lois Housman, were "clean-up women and welders. I never saw any that run a jackhammer. And there were burners, stationary burners. I didn't see anybody that was dragging a hose around over the deck. Just stationary burners – not on the ship – and welders, that's all."[6]

Government and industry used what Ruth Milkman has called the "idiom of sex typing" to explain the differences between men's and women's jobs in the shipyards. As in the automotive industry that Milkman studied, women were associated with "'light,' 'repetitive' work, demanding manual 'dexterity.'"[7] The directive ordering the admission of women into the Boilermakers union, for example, noted the "necessity for the induction of women into the lighter jobs for which they are able to qualify."[8] Government, industry, and labor agreed that not all shipyard jobs were suitable for women. While the

Table 1. Male and Female Workers by Classification at the Three Kaiser Yards, Week of October 16, 1943.

CLASSIFICATIONS	MEN	WOMEN	PERCENT OF WOMEN IN EACH CLASS
Blacksmiths	116	0	0
Shipwrights	3,298	2	.008
Chippers	2,757	4	.02
Sheetmetal workers	922	62	.257
Pipefitters	5,586	88	.365
Riggers	2,645	92	.38
Painters	2,186	129	.535
Machinists	4,169	185	.76
Boilermakers	2,757	213	.88
Shipfitters	6,888	368	.06
Laborers	80	359	1.49
Welder trainees	544	493	2.04
Electricians	3,650	557	2.3
Miscellaneous[a]	6,013	853	3.54
Warehousemen	1,228	1,115	4.62
Burners	3,076	1,214	5.03
Welders	9,676	5,218	21.60
Exempt and clerical workers	4,519	5,356	22.22
General helpers	5,477	7,597	31.52
Total workers	65,811	24,105	26.8

Source: "Combined Report of Labor Requirements," records of the U.S. Maritime Commission, R.G. 178, N.A.

[a]Includes guards and all other yard labor classification.

Women's Bureau attempted to establish some empirical basis for making such distinctions, the actual assignment of work was dictated mainly by expediency and sex stereotypes. One of the aims of the Women's Bureau publication *Employing Women in the Shipyards* by Dorothy Newman (hereafter referred to as Shipyard Survey) was to give managers guidance in the assignment of women to shipyard jobs. Newman recommended a detailed analysis of each job to determine the skill, effort, and training it required and the dangers it entailed. Such job analyses could then be used to determine the suitability of jobs for women and changes that could be made to adapt the job to women's needs. While acknowledging that "the best criterion for good placement is not one of sex but of the individual's ability to do the work successfully and without injury," she invoked physiology in recommending the assignment and modification of jobs for women. Newman urged employers to recognize that

> The frame of a woman is such that it is more difficult for her than for a man to maintain her balance; that a woman's blood has a higher water content than a man's and contains up to 20 percent fewer red corpuscles; that her heart beats about eighty times more a minute, and her muscles, proportionately longer and thinner, allow her a squeeze only about three-fifths of a man's. Physiology shows, therefore, that a woman is not only less strong muscularly, but, because of the blood and heart difference, she tends to tire more quickly than a man. Besides these considerations, persons responsible for placement will want to take into account that women's average height is 5 inches less than that of men; their reach is less; their fingers and hands are smaller; and because they are more likely to get varicose veins and tire more quickly, constant standing is more difficult for them.[9]

According to Newman, steel bucking up, caulking, heavy bus and truck driving, and heavy, dirty ship and tank cleaning were jobs for which "only exceptional woman and even the above average man can qualify," and she cautioned that women should never do work that involved pneumatic tools.[10]

Shipyard managements had expressed interest in the Women's Bureau's guidelines, but there is no evidence that these considerations dictated the distribution of women in the Portland and Vancouver yards.[11] The Women's Bureau Shipyard Survey revealed that in shipyards throughout the country "employment of women in the shipyards went ahead most quickly in the fields where most workers were urgently needed without due regard for meeting the requirements of the job with the properly qualified person."[12]

The Women's Bureau's efforts to apply their analysis of shipyard jobs to the utilization of women workers in the Kaiser yards was frustrated by the Kaiser management and the national War Manpower Commission. When, in April 1943, Saidie Dunbar, a member of the Women's Advisory Committee to the War Manpower Commission, reported on "very bad conditions" at the Kaiser yards in Portland, the War Manpower Commission decided to send Sara Southall, a personnel officer at International Harvester, to investigate, assisted by Thelma McKelvey, a War Manpower Commission staff member. Although Southall asked them for assistance, the Women's Bureau staff were irritated that they were not asked to do the investigation themselves and saw the incident as one of many examples in which the War Manpower Commission ignored their expertise.[13] They tried to arrange for Margaret Kay Anderson and Jennie Mohr of the West Coast Women's Bureau office to meet McKelvey and Southall in Portland, but the arrangements did not work out. Evidently Lee Stoll and Ann Treadwell of the regional War Manpower Commission supported the Women's Bureau and planned to give Southall and McKelvey "the bum's rush" and have the Women's Bureau staff come up later and do "a real job."[14] Southall and McKelvey flew out, were given a grand tour complete with launching, but were rushed through the yards. When they returned to Washington they wrote a report that made general recommendations about ways to "increase the efficiency of the women workers, lower absenteeism and turnover and move towards the stabilization of this portion of the shipyard workforce." Despite the fact that the Women's Advisory Committee and the Women's Bureau had expressed their concern about women doing "very heavy work," Southall and McKelvey made no recommendations about the assignment of women to shipyard jobs.[15] Ann Treadwell, of the regional War Manpower Commission, reported that during their visit "things had taken a very strange turn" and that the Kaiser management was "no longer anxious to have anything constructive done" in the yards. In her view, the "whole attempt at working out a model labor utilization study was a complete failure."[16]

The distinguishing characteristic of the jobs for which women were being recruited was neither their lightness, the need for manual dexterity, nor the considerations outlined by Newman. Women were hired mainly as helpers, jobs which required less training and received less pay. More women achieved journeyman status in welding than in other shipyard crafts because of the acute shortage of welders and the relatively short training period required.[17]

In fact, much of the heavy and dirty cleaning was performed by women. In May 1943, for example, 65 percent of the cleaners at Swan Island were women, and tank cleaning, the most undesirable job in the yards, was frequently performed by all-women crews.[18] The caption under a picture of a crew of twenty-nine women tank cleaners at Commercial Iron Works read: "Too smelly and too dirty for men."[19] The association of women with domestic work also proved to be a more powerful determinant of job distribution than the complex physiological guidelines of the Women's Bureau. In May 1943, 1,000 women and 414 men could be found among the sweepers at Swan Island. The *Bo's'n's Whistle* reported, "In the plate shop all new women employees start with the crew of 150 women who sweep and clean up that area. Regardless of experience or ultimate job desired, if the new employee is a woman, her first job is sweeping."[20]

The sexual caste system was also reproduced in the hierarchy of the shipyard workforce. Lead men were predominantly male, and forewomen were rare. At Swan Island, for example, in August 1943, when women were 27 percent of the industrial work force, only 1 of the 333 foremen was a woman and only 45 of 1,500 lead men were women.[21] "I don't recall seeing women in the jobs as leaders or supervisors," recalled Doris Avshalomov, "except the sweepers! There was a woman supervisor of the sweepers."[22] The only woman interviewed who had been a lead woman was Mabel Davis, who led a crew of tank cleaners.[23] Reva Baker, however, was performing lead man's work without the commensurate pay or title.

> At that time they had men who went around and inspected welding from the shipyards for the maritime men and if the welds weren't what they should be they'd mark with a yellow pencil around them and then they'd have a chipper come in and chip that part of the welding out and reweld it if it didn't look good. And so this man asked me if I'd like to do that. I said well, yes, so he showed me how to do it and what to look for, and I did it and he said he was gonna try to get me the title because it would be like a lead man's title; it was a higher-paying job than a welding job. Well, he chickened out.[24]

Tank cleaning crew at commercial iron works. *Courtesy of the Oregon Historical Society, negative #64477.*

Baker's situation was evidently not unique. The Shipyard Survey found rampant discrimination in the upgrading of women and many cases of women working in supervisory positions without receiving the appropriate wage or status. Newman saw this problem as a legacy of the job breakdown that had occurred in the shipbuilding industry. As Deborah Hirshfield has pointed out, shipbuilding was transformed from a craft-based to a mass-production-based industry in order to facilitate the rapid production of ships.[25] Jobs that had previously involved from forty to seventy separate operations and required four to five years' apprenticeship were broken down into specialized skills for which new workers, both male and female, could be trained in three to four weeks. Workers were often upgraded to supervisory positions that had taken years to achieve in the prewar world. Craft unions cooperated with the skill dilution because the shipbuilding boom swelled union treasuries, mechanic wage rates were maintained, and the closed shop protected the unions.[26] According to Newman, however, individual workers were threatened by the "90-day wonders" of the shipyard and resisted upgrading them to top wage rates.[27]

Reva Baker, however, saw her experience as part of the sexual hierarchy of the shipyard, and she was so distressed by the refusal of her supervisor to pay her for the work she was doing that she quit her shipyard job.

Because those days women weren't allowed to be over men and I basically would have been checking on men's work. And the other men told me too that he wouldn't back me up, that as long as I did it and did a good job I could do it on welders' pay. So I faced him on it one day. He said he was sorry but he . . . knew that they wouldn't go along with it. And they probably wouldn't – the bosses. They wouldn't accept a woman in that position because those days they didn't. We were allowed to do the basic work but none of the boss jobs, none of the lead jobs.[28]

The Shipyard Survey also found many women working in more highly skilled positions than they were being paid for.[29] Beatrice Hadley and Edna Hopkins were both victims of this form of discrimination. Both were doing certified welding, a form of welding that required special tests and received higher pay. Neither of them considered the course of action that Reva Baker chose, but both were aware of the injustice. "I asked," remembers Edna Hopkins, "'Am I doing certified welding?' . . . 'No, Shorty, you're not.' But I was, and I knew it, but there wasn't anything I could do about it. You had to do the work they brought you."[30]

A variety of factors combined to inhibit resistance to the limited options available to women: the lack of experience most women had with collective action, the knowledge that even without the salary increase women were making more money than they ever had, and the assumption that sex discrimination was part of life. Edna Hopkins's husband, who had been active in the Congress of Industrial Organizations (CIO) in the Appalachian mining town where they lived before the war, was outraged when he discovered that Edna was doing work she wasn't paid for. Edna, however, was resigned to what she saw as unchangeable and didn't want to lose her job. Beatrice Hadley commented that if she had been the only women who had been treated this way she would have been upset but "due to the fact that they weren't certifying women, why of course, it didn't bother me."[31] Reva Baker was outraged, but the only method of protest that she saw available to her was to quit her job.

Black Women in the Shipyards

In April 1944 Margaret Bernard, an Alabama black woman, wrote to the Fair Employment Practices Committee complaining about racial discrimination in southern shipyards. "I would like to go to Tuskegee to learn Welding and Burning," Bernard wrote, "but I know if I did I would have to go up North in order to Weld or Burn."[32]

Margaret Bernard would have been disappointed if she had come north to the Portland and Vancouver shipyards. Racism pervaded the shipyards and the community. Black workers were attracted to the promise of shipyard jobs, but while the black population of Portland grew from 1,934 in 1940 to 22,000 at its wartime peak, racial discrimination remained a problem throughout the war.

Discriminatory practices limited the number of black workers who gained access to skilled jobs. While the unions of unskilled workers admitted blacks, the International Brotherhood of Electrical Workers was the only union representing skilled workers that admitted black workers on an equal basis. The Boilermakers union established a separate black auxiliary whose members were not entitled to full union privileges, and the Kaiser management cooperated in firing workers who refused to join the black union. A group of black men filed a complaint with the Fair Employment Practice Committee (FEPC) against the Boilermakers and the shipyard managements. After two sets of hearings, The FEPC concluded that both the union and management were guilty of discriminatory practices. It directed the union to grant blacks full membership in the local and ordered management to stop discharging workers who did not belong to the segregated auxiliary. Neither the union nor management fully complied with the directives, and discriminatory practices persisted. Recognizing that the FEPC had no power to enforce its directives, black workers took the case to court. The court case was not settled until March 1945, when the shipyards and union were forced to admit black workers on an equal basis. By that time, however, the war was almost over.[33]

Statistics on the distribution of black workers in the yards vary wildly. While the Kaiser management maintained, during the FEPC hearings, that 70 percent of the black workers in their yards were journeymen, a researcher estimated in 1943 that 89 percent of all black shipyard workers were helpers and laborers.[34]

Statistics for the distribution of black women by craft and grade are available only for Kaiser Vancouver, which the Kaiser management highlighted during the FEPC trials since it hired the most black workers of the three Kaiser yards. Evidence from the shipyard newspapers, oral history interviews and the files of the FEPC strongly suggest that black women had even more difficulty penetrating the skilled trades than black men.[35] Even the statistics of the Kaiser management for the Vancouver yard, which make no distinction between helper and journeyman, show that while women composed 31 percent of the black work force in 1943, they composed only 20 percent of black welders, 21 percent of black electricians, and a tiny percentage of the other skilled trades.[36]

Virginia Lemire, the coordinator of women's services for the three Kaiser yards and the assistant personnel manager at Swan Island, claimed at the FEPC Hearings in November 1943 that black women were concentrated in unskilled jobs because most of them were unqualified and unsuited for skilled work.[37] Both oral history recollections and the records of the Fair Employment Practice Committee demonstrate however, that black women were barred from skilled work regardless of qualifications or training.

Beatrice Marshall, her sister, and her two friends were trained as steel-lathe and drill-press operators in a National Youth Administration (NYA) program in South Bend, Indiana, one of the several thousand NYA training programs that had been geared to meet the demands of defense industries for trained workers.[38] Marshall loved learning to use machines. "I felt like I was a champion on the drill press, and I really did like it," she commented. The NYA paid the four women's train fare to Portland and put them up for the first night at the YWCA. They had brought their papers certifying that they had passed their tests in Indiana, and they were looking forward with excitement to working as shipyard machinists. Their hopes however, were soon dashed. "When we got to the shipyards, ready to apply for the work," Marshall recalled,

> they told us that they didn't have any openings as lathe or drill-press operators; and that we would have to either accept painter's helper or a sweeper. . . . And we complained because that wasn't what we was trained for. And we asked for a job with what we was trained for. And they said it wasn't any available.[39]

After some persistance, Marshall and her friends got the personnel office to admit that there were openings in the machine shop but that they were not accepting black workers. Statistics collected in 1943 show fifty black machinists working in the shipyards, but none of them were women.[40] Marshall and her friends complained to the newly organized chapter of the Urban League but were unsuccessful in gaining admission to the machine shop, so they worked for a while as unskilled laborers and then left the shipyards. Marshall was hurt, angry, and confused. "They was doing all this advertising and wanting us to do this, and here I am spending time and getting trained and qualified and couldn't get it. . . . I was real mad."[41]

The shipyards' failure to upgrade black women shipyard workers also elicited complaints. Maude Robinson sent a telegram to President Roosevelt in July 1944 asking for an investigation of the Swan Island Shipyards where, she claimed, "transfer from scaler to painter," is refused any colored girl regardless of length of service or good record." According to Robinson, white women were transferred to the paint shop after scaling only a few weeks, while black women who had been scalers for seven months or more were refused transfer. Investigation revealed that there were no black women working in the paint shop, but the shipyard management denied that this was the result of discrimination, and the Fair Employment Practice Committee dismissed the case.[42]

Some black women did achieve journeyman status, mostly as welders, but their positions as skilled workers could be precarious. In the spring of 1944 six women welders at Kaiser Vancouver went to the War Manpower Commission to protest against what they felt were discriminatory discharges.[43] The six women, who had been working on the graveyard shift, had complained to the supervisor about their lead man, who had routinely addressed them as "niggers" and treated them unfairly.[44] The lead man was demoted to journeyman, but the women were all transferred to swing shift with no explanation. They had all made it clear that they cared for children and had arranged child care to accommodate the graveyard shift. After working on swing shift for a short time, the women were given discharge notices and told they could only work day shift. "I told them," wrote Doris Mae Williams," it would be impossible to work days with two small children, one school age and the other too young to attend a nursery, my husband gone to service . . . but my request went unheeded." The women either quit or took jobs as laborers in order to work the graveyard shift. "I am now scaling – hard labor," wrote Williams to the FEPC. "Our crew is mixed, we are all treated alike. Why couldn't the same be said for skilled workers?"[45] The FEPC investigated the case, but the management of Kaiser Vancouver claimed that the women were fired for loafing. The FEPC, feeling that "there was no concrete evidence to go on," dismissed the case.[46] The women belonged to Local 32, the segregated auxiliary that had been established for black workers, and the local black newspaper cited the local's failure to defend the women as an example of the weakness of segregated unions.[47]

A Satisfying Job

The jobs that Marshall called "unskilled and unwanted work" were arduous and routine and few narrators remembered them as personally fullfilling. After being rejected as machinists and given a choice between painter's helper and sweeper, Marshall and her friends chose "painter's helper" because it seemed like it would be more interesting than sweeping.

> To our surprise, it was something we really wished a thousand times we hadn't taken, because the job was in the bottom of the boat. . . . We had to go through . . . little round holes that was made. And we had to crawl on our hands and knees and carry our light on an extension cord to see because it was pitch dark in there. And we had a little tool, something like a spreader, where we scraped the rust off the bottom of the boat where they had to paint. . . . We had to wear masks, there so much rust in there until you could hardly breathe.[48]

The women whose jobs involved learning new skills, however, did describe a sense of personal development. For the many women who came to shipyard work from traditionally female work the shipyard often provided a welcome contrast. It would be a mistake to romanticize blue-collar work, particularly work that, like shipbuilding, had been substantially "deskilled." It did, however, have a number of features that distinguished it from traditionally female work. A brief discussion of five of the narrators who mentioned that contrast will illustrate these differences.

Virginia Larson and Loena Ellis had both been working in factories before the war: Ellis at a bag factory and Larson at a linen mill. Both noted the contrast between their prewar jobs and work at the shipyard. Larson, who described textile work as tedious and pressured, felt that as a machinist in the shipyard she was "accomplishing something."[49] Ellis compared the activity of the shipyard with the monotony of the bag factory. She also felt more interested in what she was doing in the shipyard. "There's something about a ship," she commented, "even when it's being built, that has a fascination to it." Reva Baker, who had been working as a domestic before the war, spoke of a sense of accomplishment in shipbuilding. "It's very exciting," she said, "to see that ship slip down the ways, after you've been working on it."[50] Joanne Hudlicky, who had been working at a cigar store, appreciated the physical challenge of crane operating, and LueRayne Culbertson, who had been a waitress, commented on the creative aspects of welding. "When you chip that slag off and see that gorgeous weld underneath – no undercuts, no nothing – just a beautiful weld – it was a real, real satisfying job."[51]

Despite the dominant pattern of sex segregation, there *were* women who crossed the boundaries that divided women's and men's work in the wartime shipyards. War Manpower Commission records reveal that small numbers of women did achieve journeyman status in fields other than welding in the Kaiser shipyards in 1943 (see table 2). Behind these numbers were the stories of women who actively shaped their work lives by pursuing occupations they thought would be satisfying. Women's entry into crafts besides welding was not facilitated by active recruitment and required taking the initiative. The presence of women in these crafts demonstrates that some women, perhaps emboldened by the sense of capability they developed in the shipyards, pushed open doors that were slightly ajar and challenged the limits they found in the shipyard world.

Joanne Hudlicky, for example, became one of the few women crane operators at Oregon Shipbuilding Corporation. Hudlicky, originally hired to work in the clearance office, described the process by which she became a crane operator.

> I worked in the clearance office and that's an office where the people that have either been laid off, quit, or fired come through. And I

Welders at Oregon Shipbuilding Corporation. *Courtesy of the Oregon Historical Society, negative #CN020092.*

didn't like office work, I never did. So when they were coming through there and I found out how much money they were making, I decided that I would quit and go down and hire out as a helper. And I hired out as a helper and I went to work duplicating – now that's climbing up on plates, steel plates – and you have a hammer and a big heavy metal nail . . . and you had to hammer on little dots. And I

Table 2. Women Journeymen at the Kaiser Yard

	SWAN ISLAND (8/43)	OSC (12/43)	KAISER VANCOUVER (11/43)
Burners	178	75	345
Crane operators	(none given)	10	(none given)
Electricians	113	75	345
Painters	50	18	205
Shipfitters	197	6	56
Drillers	(none given)	1	10
Machinists	62	1	55
Sheetmetal workers	12	(none given)	31
Layers out	(none given)	2	(none given)
Expediters	(none given)	45	89
Welders	1,810	1,148	1,227

Source: U.S. War Manpower Commission, *Survey of Shipyard Operations in the Portland, Oregon Metropolitan Area*, Vols. 1, 2 and 3, Portland, 1943.

didn't like that either and I said, "How do you get a job running a crane?" And he said, "Well, you have to talk to the man that hires for that." . . . Well evidently he told him about me, because the next day he came around and said, "I hear you'd like to run a crane." And I said, "I sure would." And he said, "Do you think you can do that?" I said, "Well, I don't know why not; other people are doing it." And the very next day he came after me.[52]

Hudlicky loved crane operating and thinks that part of its appeal was that "it was something that we weren't allowed to do before."[53] She had been frustrated by the limited opportunities for women in sports in high school and felt that crane operating came close to the challenge she experienced in sports. The wartime situation made it possible for her to do something for which she felt a natural affinity. The opportunity came, however, because she noticed and pursued it.

Table 2 indicates that there were no women drillers at Swan Island in August 1943. Although she does not remember the date, Alice Erickson remembers well the story of how she became a driller at Swan Island.

I was working; I was what they called a tack welder. I was welding just the tack welds for the shipfitters and I was interested, I watched these guys on these drills and I just thought that it would be interesting to operate one of those big drills. . . . When I asked to try out on the drill, he looked at me kind of funny and he said, "Well, I've never had a woman driller on my crew." "Well, I think I can handle it." So he allowed me to try out.[54]

Erickson worked as a driller until the end of the war.[50]

Both oral and written sources offer glimpses of other attempts by women to control their work lives. Female welders sometimes worked on all-women crews and sometimes on mixed crews. One all-women crew protested an attempt to disperse them and convinced the shipyard management that such a move would "wreck their efficiency."[55] Ree Adkins and Frankie Cooper changed jobs as often as they could in an effort to remain challenged. "I'd stay on a crew so long," recalled Cooper "and I'd say, Oh, I want to be transferred 'cause I want to learn how to do this heavy welding or I want to learn how to do this impossible welding, you know, that they say is so hard to do. So that's what I did, I just transferred all over the boat."[56] When Etta Harvey, a burner, felt frustrated by a lead man who would not give women challenging work, she maneuvered her way into another crew. After that, she reported, "I was perfectly happy 'cause I had, you know, work that I enjoyed and felt I was contributing to something."[57]

The shipyard world that women industrial workers found during the war was in some ways, a radical departure from normalcy. In other ways, shipyard life echoed the customary patterns of sexual and racial inequity, patterns that women accepted at times and challenged at other times. While women were never fully integrated into the shipyard work force, some women, particularly those doing skilled work, found satisfaction and challenge in shipyard work, and some pushed against the limits that constrained them in order to enrich their work experience.

Cold Metal and Old Man Moon

"Go into the yard as a worker, not as a women," exhorted Augusta Clawson, who was sent by the Office of Education to work as a welder in the Swan Island yard and make recommendations to improve training for women. Clawson described her experiences in a popular paperback, *Diary of a Welder*, in addition to her reports to the Office of Education and the Oregon Division of the U.S. Employment Service (U.S.E.S.). She concluded one report with advice that she thought should be given to new women production workers. Heading her list was the admonition that women should not expect male workers to

Electricians at Oregon Shipbuilding corporation.   *Courtesy of the Oregon Historical Society, negative #80366.*

have chivalrous habits. "They may curse, they will not offer the courtesies that go with social contacts, they may shove past you, spit upon the decks, fill up the seats on the buses."[58]

The evidence indicates, however, that no matter how hard women tried to follow Clawson's advice, the atmosphere of the yards reminded them in myriad ways that they were female and a minority. The attitudes of male workers, the columnists and cartoonists of the shipyard newspapers, and the management of the yards all contributed to an environment that heightened rather than minimized the differences between male and female workers. Women workers often enjoyed their work, and they usually grew accustomed to the industrial environment, but they never were allowed to forget they were women –

imposters on male territory treated as amusing toys or tolerated "for the duration."

This is not to say that all men were antagonistic to women workers. Neither contemporary observers nor the former shipyard workers described the male workers as a monolithic bloc of opposition. In a report of a conference for supervisors on the problems of women production workers, Maude Withers, of the personnel office of Iron Fireman, (a Portland company that manufactured furnaces for the ships) observed, "psychologically, it was not easy for workers and supervisors to accept women. . . . They were reluctant to admit women to a trade formerly belonging solely to them." Of the twenty supervisors attending the conference, roughly half were optimistic about training and upgrading women, and most of the others possessed some reservations and wanted to proceed with caution. Only two thought it was hopeless to try to train women to do production work well.[59]

Only one narrator, Audrey Moore, retained a dominant memory of hostility. "They always acted like they resented the women being there," she commented. "Everybody seemed to have chips on their shoulders."[60] As a black worker, Moore's memories of a hostile work environment combined racial and sexual tensions. Most narrators remembered some male workers as hostile and others as friendly. "The average of them was pretty nice," commented Nona Pool, "but there was a lot of hardheads that just didn't have enough sense to pour sand out of a boot, and they thought that women were supposed to be pregnant and barefoot and 'yes sir'."[61]

Two of the narrators (Berenice Thompson and Nell Conley) identified the older men as those who had the most difficulty accepting women workers. "They had grown up in another age," Conley pointed out. "This wasn't very much after the Depression, when any job at all meant life or death. There was no social security, there was no way people could get food if they didn't have it or couldn't pay for it, and I think that those men actually felt that we were a threat to them."[62] "There were a lot of men," agreed Berenice Thompson, "that didn't think that they [women] should be there, either, especially old gray-haired men. 'They belong home with their kids or their grandkids.' . . . They were just jealous, I think, that we could do as well as they could and better—we did better."[63] Loena Ellis, on the other hand, had the most difficulty with a young man who was her partner. "I think he looked upon working with women as sort of like having a kid sister tagging along, and he resented it. The older ones didn't so much, but this young fellow did and so he would take jobs in the most awkward places, I think, trying to lose me."[64]

The dominant memory of the women shipyard workers is of having to prove oneself. "A woman crane operator," commented Joanne Hudlicky, "had to be a little bit better, let's put it that way. There might be a man relieving for a crane operator and maybe he wasn't as good an operator as the man he was relieving but they wouldn't have cared. I put everything into it I could 'cause I really wanted to do it and I think that it's that way with a lot of women. I think I was a real good operator. I mean that's how I felt."[65] "I did think," reflected Virginia Larson, a machinist, "that they gave us a little more chores, if you know what I mean. You had to prove yourself a little more than the men. In fact, I know that to be a fact. When we graduated we had to make a little tool . . . a little vise, and they made us girls make two of them. And the guys only had to make one. And both were perfect. I remember, they both turned out perfect. I think they thought, 'Oh they're just lucky the first time,' you know. But we passed with flying colors."[66] "The first day I was out there," recalled LueRayne Culbertson, a welder, "he [the lead man – who later became her husband] told me to run this pass across on this dog they shore up the metal with and I ran one quick pass across it and he says, "Why don't you put some metal on there?' And I said, 'Well, break it off, if it doesn't hold, I'll put it on again.' He pounded that thing to death, but he couldn't get it off of there."[67] Reva Baker began her shipyard work on a crew of ten women. "We started out tack welding," she explained.

> You just put a little strip of welding on a piece of metal that's attached to either a deck or a bulkhead to hold it in place until they could do the production welding on it to make it solid. We didn't do that very long. . . . Then they thought they'd try us on production welding. . . . They didn't think that the women could do that well but they gave us a chance, we were to prove that we could do the production welding as well as the men did and we proved it to them. In fact, some of us did better than some of the men.[68]

Attitudes toward the capabilities of women workers improved with time. Mike Miller, general manager of the Swan Island yards, told the *Bos'n's Whistle* in November 1944, "If anyone had ever told me in the days of Boulder, Grand Coulee Dam, or Bonneville that the Kaiser company would be hiring women on all these jobs I would have told them they were crazy. In fact, if they expected me to manage a shipbuilding outfit this size with nearly a third of the help women, I would probably have been tempted to tell them to get somebody else to take my job. But I'm still here and the women are doing a splendid job."[69] Narrators' recollections also attest to initial hostility that abated after men and women had worked together for a while. Loena Ellis's lead man, for example, seemed to have more trouble with the idea of women workers than with the reality.

> He really kicked up a storm when he found out he was going to have to hire women on the crew. They said he really threw a tantrum. Well I couldn't imagine him throwing a tantrum till I saw him do it one day. He wore striped overalls and a striped cap, regular engineer's working outfit, and the time I saw him throw a tantrum he took that hat off, he threw it on the floor, he jumped up and down and he just turned the air blue. And that's what he did when he found out he was gonna have to have women on the crew down there because he just wasn't raised that way. But we got along fine, he was no problem after we were down there.[70]

The cartoons in the shipyard newspapers also exhibited a marked change of attitude toward women's abilities as the female production worker became a commonplace sight. While female incompetence had been a target of satire when the shipyards first began recruiting women (see chapter 1), inept women virtually disappeared from the shipyard comic strips by early 1943.[71]

But while the incompetent ninny receded to the background in the humor of the shipyard magazines, another caricature moved to the foreground – the frivolous sexpot. With protruding hips and breasts, she appeared repeatedly in cartoons in the *Bo's'n's Whistle*, *Stem to Stern*, and the *Porthole*, reminding men and women alike that underneath the welding helmet there were creatures irrevocably different from men – provocative, jealous, nagging wives and girlfriends, obsessively concerned with their looks, addicted to gossip and eternally sexual[72].

Katherine Archibald, a sociologist who wrote about her experiences in a wartime California shipyard, commented that

> whatever the degree of adjustment, whatever the outward appearance of harmony, the ancient doctrine was never wholly abandoned that the real and only power of women was the power of sex, and their sole possible contribution to the field of masculine endeavor was one of negative distraction and disturbance rather than positive aid.[73]

"Put on a shade that will go with WISCO pipe shop grease, please."

Stem to Stern, **October 7, 1943.**

Both the written record and the oral history material indicate that a similar atmosphere prevailed in the Portland and Vancouver yards and that it functioned to reinforce women's sense of themselves as alien and temporary in a male world.

In the cartoon strip "Stubby Bilgebottom," which appeared regularly in all the editions of the *Bo's'n's Whistle,* female workers are presented in two roles: causing (by their mere presence) disruption and confusion to the main character, Stubby, or, in the character of "Gertie," incurably romantic and fearful, whose very vocabulary is so full of feminine references that her presence in the shipyards seems absurd.[74] Perhaps the most revealing is the strip in which Stubby gives Gertie a jar of boot grease for Christmas. Gertie, expecting something feminine, is horrified.[75] It must have been difficult for women workers to heed Augusta Clawson's advise to see themselves as workers when surrounded by messages that reinforced the assumption that women wanted to be treated "as women."

The elaboration of the "femininity" of women workers took place on many levels. Language played an important role. Despite the fact that by April 1944 an average of 27 percent of the work force at each Kaiser shipyard was female, articles in shipyard papers describing workers in general referred only to men. In shipyard and community newspapers, male workers were identified by either their last names or both first and last names, while women were sometimes identified by first and last names but often by first names only. Women welders were often called "welderettes" or "lady welders." Of course, male workers were seldom referred to as "boys," while women workers were often called "girls."[76]

Glamour was a shipyard institution. A gallery of "pin-up" girls at Oregon Ship exhibited pictures of women shipyard workers selected by roving male "glamour detectors." All the yards staged frequent beauty and popularity contests for women workers. Articles in shipyard papers about women's achievements were often larded with detailed descriptions of their appearance, family life, and mode of dressing during off-hours. For example, a photo essay about the winner of a national women's welding contest was entitled "Welding Champ No Wizard: Just Ordinary Girl." The purpose of the piece was the "prove Joy Wilson, 21-year-old East and West Coast welder champion, is a natural American girl and not a mechanical wizard who spends her evenings practicing with a stinger and welding machine in her basement." The lead picture in the essay is a full-length photograph of Wilson in a bathing suit with a caption reading (in part), "Here's evidence that a girl can work all day in the shipyard and still be glamorous." The other photographs picture Wilson reading a novel, getting out of the bathtub, and cooking breakfast for herself and her brother. There is one picture of Wilson welding.[77]

An article in *The Oregonian*'s Sunday magazine crooned, "It seems that the maidens who work on the day and swing shifts are all cold business. But not so the graveyard gals. They can apply themselves to cold metal just so long. They've just naturally got to gaze upward through the rafters of the assembly bay for another glimpse of Old Man Moon. Their eyes get soft, their glances stray. They sigh."[78] In her book on sexual harassment in the workplace, Lin Farley notes that painting a picture of women as perpetually sexual reinforces "the right of men to harass, control and/or abuse working women sexually. It accomplishes this by undermining women's role as worker, then reinforcing their use as sex objects by implying that they invite it. The

STUBBY BILGEBOTTOM · · · · · **by Ernie Hager**

Bo's'n's Whistle, June 3, 1943.   Courtesy of the Oregon Historical Society.

Bo's'n's Whistle, July 6, 1945.   Courtesy of the Oregon Historical Society.

message is conveyed that if women are going to make themselves sexual game, men have a license, even an obligation, to hunt."[79]

Legal precedent has in fact recently defined an atmosphere in which women are routinely treated as sexual objects as a form of sexual harassment and connected it with sexual harassment's more overt form – the use of power at the workplace to pressure an individual into sexual activity. The wartime shipyards demonstrate both the connection between these two kinds of harassment and the difference between them. All of the women interviewed who experienced the narrower form of sexual harassment were outraged and did what they could to avoid or stop it. Responses to the broader form of sexual harassment – the pervasive emphasis on femininity and sexual appeal – were more varied.

Doris Avshalomov found the sexual attention disconcerting.

> I remember one night I wasn't wearing my hard hat and this one guy came up to me and he said, "Your hair is driving me crazy." And I said, "Yeah, I know, I should have my hard hat on." I thought he was worried about my safety. And he said, "Oh no, no, no, I just love to see it!" And so I guess that having women on the ships was just more than the men could deal with. You know, I'm just generalizing. But I was aware of it, and it made me a little bit uncomfortable.[80]

Avshalomov felt similarly uncomfortable about her participation in a beauty contest.

> I remember that beauty contest. I was really embarrassed about the whole thing. But my crew were so proud that I was chosen that I had to go represent them. And I felt that that was very demeaning, I really did. . . . What we had to do was prance on the stage and be interviewed and . . . then have our pictures taken. It was very simple. But I remember the man who interviewed us asked such stupid questions and seemed so opinionated. And as I walked on – I was tall and had kind of an energetic stride – he said, "Here comes Rosie the Riveter." And I pointed out that I wasn't a riveter, I was an electrician. I mean, my enthusiasm dropped right then and there. . . . It didn't really, in my opinion, contribute to the war effort.[81]

But Avshalomov's view of the war effort was not the prevailing one. Glamorous images of women workers appeared throughout the country. Cosmetics did not require a priority number in the wartime rationing system because "the government believes cosmetics aid in building morale and consequently will not cut down seriously on production."[82]

Bo's'n's Whistle, **March 31, 1944.** *Courtesy of the Oregon Historical Society.*

"Yeah, busy little bee all right—she's been tryin' to open her compact for the past hour!"

Bo's'n's Whistle, **July 28, 1944.** *Courtesy of the Oregon Historical Society.*

Did you happen to see a little bottle of "Night of Moonbeams and Ecstasy?"

Bo's'n's Whistle, July 14, 1944.   *Courtesy of the Oregon Historical Society.*

. . . "It looks something like a big hairpin with a doojigger like a perfume bottle cap on it!"

Bo's'n's Whistle, August 11, 1944.   *Courtesy of the Oregon Historical Society.*

Stubby Bilgebottom   **By Ernie Hager**

Bo's'n's Whistle, December 22, 1944. *Courtesy of the Oregon Historical Society.*

There were other glimmers of dissent from the general obsession with female attractiveness, particularly when it resulted in the neglect of women's real experience and needs. Nell Conley remembers feeling impatient with the frequent shipyard fashion shows. Irritated by the preparations for a show at Oregon Ship directed by a Hollywood designer, Conley registered her objections:

> I thought, Goddamn foolishness for women who only want decent clothes to work in to bring that kind of thing here, so I fussed a bit. And I had a friend who was on the counseling staff. . . . I talked to her about my dissatisfaction with fashion shows and she suggested to

the powers that were at the time that perhaps a welding style show would be a good idea. "Well, if you can find something to show we'll show it." So I went to all the stores in town that sold welding clothing and told them what we wanted, and somehow or other they came up with some women's outfits.[83]

As a result of Conley's efforts a fashion show of work clothes for women was held at Oregon Ship in November 1942. Six outfits found in local shops were modeled by women shipyard workers in different jobs.[84] During the following summer the Women's Bureau, the Safety Association, and the Kaiser management brought a fashion designer to the shipyards who developed a line of "fleet fashions" suitable for shipyard work in the weather conditions of the Pacific Northwest.[85]

A poem that appeared in the *Bo's'n's Whistle* objected to the connection between sex appeal and recognition at the shipyards. The headline read, "Unglamorous Women Glorified by Swan Poet," and the poem, written by Iva Brustman, age fifty-two, was entitled "Preserved Cogs." In satirical doggerel it called attention to the existence of older women workers, a sizable portion of the labor force, and concluded:

So, call us the "Biddies" or "Old Hens" if you
    will,
We've done a great job, and we're doing it still
As long as we work and send our boys plenty,
They won't give a D— — if we're forty or twenty![86]

Etta Harvey was distressed by the way that the sexually charged atmosphere inhibited camaraderie between male and female workers. Harvey was grateful for the assistance she had received from an older man who was in charge of the training pit and upset that her co-workers imbued his attentions with sexual meaning.

So his birthday rolled around and I made the suggestion that we give him something for his birthday and took up a little collection. And they made a snide remark about my boyfriend ('cause I did spend a lot of time in the pit, but I was there to learn and not to play around) and that hurt me, too, because I wasn't dumb enough but what I knew what they were thinking and it made me feel badly.[87]

The question of work clothing embodied the conflicting attitudes toward female sexuality at work in the war industry. *Business Week* commended war industries for their "pioneering job in evolving a type

The grandmother crew, October 1944. *Courtesy of the Oregon Historical Society.*

of attire which will protect the girls from industrial accident and de-emphasize their allure without sacrificing that feminine charm which is woman's birthright."[94] When Betty Cleator was hired as a drafts-man she was asked by the foreman to wear slacks because, he said, "you'd be surprised how much time is wasted while the boys back there enjoy the girls with their skirts on the high stools."[95]

The suggestions of The Women's Bureau Shipyard Survey to avert the "so called 'moral problem'" reflected this focus on women's behavior and clothing as the source of disruptive sexual energy: only mature women should be selected for employment, women should work in groups, women should be more carefully supervised than men, and a woman counselor should be available.[96] The Women's Bureau made no suggestions for measures to control or monitor male behavior.

The assumption that women were responsible for male sexual behavior shaped the way sexual harassment was dealt with, particu-larly when supervisors were involved. Of the seven instances of sexual harassment mentioned by narrators, four involved supervisors and three involved co-workers. The narrators dealt with sexual harass-ment in the yards in a variety of ways. Sometimes they responded assertively in defense of themselves and other women, other times they sought help from administrative staff, sometimes they "man-aged" the situation, and sometimes, in Avshalomov's words, they "suf-fered in silence."[97] Most women seemed reconciled to the necessity of remaining vigilant, always aware of the possible danger and ready to cope with it in whatever ways they could.

Sometimes lead men punished women who resisted their advances by sending them into the rain to work, which, for welders, meant being exposed to repeated electric shocks. Jean Clark, who was sixteen at the time, worked in the rain for a while after refusing to "cooperate" with her lead man. "After so many shocks like that you begin to feel pretty rotten, and I finally got so tired of it that I finally told the foreman, and he just acted like it was my fault if anything happened so I better be quiet or lose my job."[98] She endured the shocks as long as she could and then asked to be assigned to a different job. She didn't want to work on the ways because "there were so few women down there and so many men," so she was unable to continue welding. Her new job was handing out plumbing accessories, and she felt safer because she was working among women. Her experience illustrates Farley's contention that "job segregation by sex is to a large extent sustained by sexual harassment."[99]

The emphasis on female sexuality heightened the undercurrent of tension about relations between white women and black men that lurked near the surface in both the shipyard and the community. *Business Week*, in reporting the discovery that fifty women were working as prostitutes in a Portland shipyard in 1942, cited a Portland policeman who was concerned that if white prostitutes consorted with Negro workers they might encourage black workers "to take liberties with white women," which might lead to "serious race complications."[88] When Clarence Williams, a black worker at Swan Island, gave a Christmas card to a white woman on his crew, his foreman said to him, "I am going to show you about buying white women presents," and had him discharged.[89]

At the FEPC hearings, Elmer Hann, general supervisor at Swan Island, testified that white women were afraid to work with black male workers. "They really don't know, I guess, what they are afraid of, it just seems to be the inborn nature of a woman and lack of social contact, perhaps, that makes them just a little reticent to be isolated with these people."[90] But white women attempting to increase their social contact with black men in the yards or the community raised eyebrows and could provoke repercussions. After an interracial dance in Vanport, one of the few racially integrated housing projects in the city, the police issued a warning to white women who had been seen dancing with black men that continuing this practice might lead to a race riot.[91] Doris Avshalomov often had lunch with a friend from Reed College and some black students from a southern college.

Some of the white workers would sort of come by and make comments at us – noises. And one night they pulled the lights out of the place where we were sitting. You know, just real annoying things. And finally, my crew leader told me that his superior wanted to talk to me. And his superior – I will give him credit, he was embarrassed, but he said that some people misunderstood the fact that I was just having lunch with these people, and that he just thought we should all just join hands and put our shoulder to the wheel and avoid any kind of disturbance of that sort. And I was just furious. . . . It was just a sort of comradely thing. The only people who ever made unwelcome advances to me were white men in the shipyards – but I didn't see my leaderman talking to me about that![92]

The shipyard atmosphere and the structure of power in the yards interacted to foster sexual harassment by white men. Women remained a minority in the yards throughout the war and most women workers had male supervisors. Predictably, information about sexual harassment is found only in the oral history material, since the subject remained unnamed and unchallenged until the 1970s. When sexual interaction between men and women *was* discussed publicly, it was treated as an inevitable by-product of what was often called a female "invasion" of male turf. For example, in *Business Week*'s discussion of the moral problems caused by the "infiltration of women into war plants," it was clear that if anyone was to blame in this inherently dangerous situation it was "the efficiency-sapping influence of the flirtatious gesture, the tight sweater, the receding hem."[93]

When management did intervene on behalf of a woman who was being sexually harassed by a supervisor or teacher, the solution was to transfer the women to another area or supervisor. When Mabel Studebaker objected to being "petted" by the foreman, who "thought he was a ladies' man," she also was ordered to work in the rain. When she refused, pointing out that new workers were normally given that assignment and she was no longer new, he replied, 'Either work out in the rain or go home.' So I went home." Studebaker returned to work, was reassigned to the same foreman, and finally, after reporting the incident to a supervisor, was transferred to another area.[100] When Kathryn Blair's lead man tried to embrace her every morning in their carpool she found his behavior "quite shocking," but aware of her vulnerable situation, she managed as adroitly as she could to hold him off without antagonizing him.[101]

Lois Housman was able to get a lead man reprimanded for sexual harassment when she intervened on behalf of another woman who refused to "flirt with" or "play with" her instructor.

He wouldn't do nothing for her. He wouldn't teach her anything and she was just crying to me like her heart would break. . . . So I went to the office and I told 'em, "She works and she's honest and she wants to work, and he won't show her nothing. And she's crying out there." And so they came out there and, boy, they sure got after him and gave her another man to teach her. And I seen her when we got out on the ways and she was an awful good welder.[102]

There were a few more options open to women who were harassed by their fellow workers rather than by their bosses. LueRayne Culbertson was able to get "Whitey" fired when she reported that he was always "copping a feel or doing something else."[103] But often women were made to feel that the norms of shipyard behavior were set by men and were violated at one's peril. Doris Avshalomov, for example, told "them very loudly to cut it out" when male workers tried to back her into a corner and touch her. "And then when they'd see me they'd make little noises and catcalls implying that I was a prude. . . . It wasn't anything I couldn't deal with but I was rather annoyed by it – especially the humiliation of being made fun of afterward."[104]

Loena Ellis's approach seems to have been more effective: "This fellow came up and took hold of my ankle and without even thinking I just brought that hammer right down on his hard hat and knocked his glasses off and broke them. That's the only time anybody ever tried anything."[105]

Female sexuality was simultaneously an object of ridicule, fascination, and uneasiness in the shipyards. The pervasive emphasis on sexuality may have been viewed as a method of easing the tensions created by women's presence in the shipyards. While some women recognized that this defusing of tension was at the expense of women's dignity as workers, there was neither the language nor the organizational means to challenge it.

3 ☆ WELDING THE SEAMS
OF THE DOUBLE DAY

A cartoon in *Stem to Stern* newspaper featured one woman worker saying to another, "What am I doing tonight? Just a few chores at home – washing the dishes, waxing the floors – then I'll come over for a chat."[1] In another cartoon in the same newspaper, a woman dressed in work clothes barked at her husband, "And another thing – you have dinner ready on time tonight or I'll knock your block off."[2]

These two cartoons illustrate two features of the wartime atmosphere: women's domestic responsibilities received more public recognition than ever before but the specter of role reversal haunted wartime humor, which hinted ominously at the disruption of power relations in the home. Government and industry publicly acknowledged the problems posed by what was then called "women's dual responsibilities" but, as several studies have documented, their responses were ambivalent, inconsistent, and inadequate. In the Portland-Vancouver area, home of the world-famous Kaiser Child Service Centers, industry took more responsibility than elsewhere for dealing with women's dual responsibilities, but measures were still fraught with controversy – and were clearly temporary.[3]

A general consensus prevailed in the periodical literature of the community and the workplace that women would remain responsible for domestic work, but fear was often expressed that women's wartime work would upset the division of labor in the home, threatening the stability of the family and the welfare of children. In general, the ideology that equated femininity with domesticity was alive and well during the war, reinforcing the sense that domestic work would always remain women's terrain. Even the question of husbands helping out with housework sometimes sparked controversy. The *Bo's'n's Whistle* at Swan Island, for example, devoted a "Roving Reporter" column to the question of housework, asking workers: "If husband and wife are both working, should the husband help with the housework?" Of the three male and three female respondents, only one – a woman – was completely negative. The others advocated varying

65

levels of male involvement in housework, from washing dishes to sharing equally, but two of these added that in normal times women should not be working. No one challenged the questioner's assumption that women would retain primary responsibility and men would "help."[4]

Augusta Clawson commented after a short time on the job, "It was very exhilirating being part of the gang, but I'm glad I don't have a husband and four children all waiting for me to cook dinner. I'm glad I don't have to do a family laundry. In fact, 'Jingle Jingle Jingle . . . thank God I'm single.'"[5]

The frenetic pace of life was a dominant memory for most of the narrators who had families at the time. One remembers taking pep pills to keep herself awake; several recall averaging three to five hours of sleep at night. For LueRayne Culbertson the pace was intensified because, uncertain about how long the defense job would last, she kept her waitress job throughout the war. She reported:

A typical workday was getting up at six in the morning, fixing breakfast, taking the baby to the Fruit and Flower mission . . . catching the bus, getting out to Oregon Ship, welding eight hours, dashing home, Pap'd pick up the baby, I'd get cleaned up and take off for my waitress job at Nendel's and he'd take care of the baby. Then I'd come home at midnight and wash out the diapers and hang them up.[6]

The counselors at the shipyards across the country were concerned about the effect of "cumulative fatigue" on women workers, and reported that women sometimes quit after working in shipyards for eight or nine months and then rehired in three or four weeks. The Swan Island Shipyard considered a policy of leave of absence for women but never implemented it.[7]

The war complicated housework in many ways. A Bryn Mawr College study on the impact of the war on women throughout the country found that war dislocations and breakdowns had increased the amount of time women spent on housework.[8] A regular women's column in *The Shipbuilder* addressed these problems as well as those presented by the demands of the double day. Services such as laundry and dry cleaning were less available, fewer appliances were being produced, and shopping often involved standing in long lines for ration coupons and scarce products. Thousands of shipyard workers lived in newly built housing projects, the largest of which, Vanport, housed 42,000 people at its peak. Inconveniences and daily harassments were multiplied in this sprawling, hastily constructed complex, which included 9,942 housing units, 181 service annexes, and 45 public buildings. Cooking had to be done on two-burner electric ranges which had an average life span of 72 hours; there were two washing machines for fifty-six families; mud was continually tracked through apartments from the many unpaved streets; and residents and staff were engaged in a constant battle with bedbugs and cockroaches. Stores were late in coming and inadequate when built, shortages were even more acute than in surrounding communities, and the only ration board was ringed by lines of people before the doors opened every morning.[9]

Marketing was difficult for all employed women because of the limited business hours of most stores. In Vancouver, community groups pressured stores to remain open at night, but the retail clerks refused, sparking a controversy that raged from March to September 1944, when the stores finally agreed to add Monday evening hours. Portland stores never extended their hours.[10]

Wartime housework was further complicated by the inflexibility of institutions which sought to prevent what they viewed as a deterioration of standards under the pressure of wartime exigencies. This often involved upholding conservative notions about gender and family life. Mabel Studebaker, for example, remembers the pressures of caring for four children while working full-time at the shipyard and her irritation with the lack of flexibility and support from her children's school.

> And at that time we had to iron, too, and of course, with three little girls I had frills to iron and dresses to iron. I did get a new coverall suit for my youngest daughter. She was in the first grade. And I thought: "it was brand-new, it was cute – she could wear it to school." And they sent her home to get a dress on. And that made me so provoked. At that time little girls didn't wear pant suits.[11]

What Should Be Done about Wage-Earning Mothers?

The role of social and educational insitutions in upholding conservative social values was a recurrent theme in the history of care for the children of employed mothers. Throughout the United States, neither state, local, or federal agencies nor private industry had much experience in dealing with the problems of wage-earning mothers. Prevailing negative attitudes toward married women wage earners precluded any consideration of services for employed mothers during the Depression. Only the nurseries run by the Works Progress Administration (WPA) provided a model for caring for the children of working parents, and they were regarded as a solution to the inevitable problems of poverty rather than a method of facilitating integration of women into the work force.

During the war there were three general approaches to the problems posed by mothers working outside the home: (1) reshape the workplace to make it more compatible with parenting, (2) discourage the employment of mothers of young children and (3) provide care for children of employed mothers.

The first approach was never taken seriously in the Portland-Vancouver area, although it was advocated by James Brunot, day-care coordinator of the Office of Community War Services in Washington, D.C., when he visited Oregon. Brunot argued for changes in the structure of industrial life in order to deal effectively with the problems of employed mothers, and he pointed to some smaller industries in New England that were experimenting with adjustment of hours, part-time employment, and split shifts.[12]

Neither Kaiser nor the smaller shipyards made any substantial changes in work schedules to accommodate workers with dual responsibilities. The only instance of a decision about working conditions made with women's domestic responsibilities in mind was at the Pacific Coast Shipbuilding Stabilization Conference in May 1944, when Lee Stoll of the War Manpower Commission took a strong position against adopting a ten-hour shift. Mary Alice Webb of the Women's Bureau, who represented Stoll on this matter, reported, "He authorized me to say to the boys at the conference that Portland's production record per man-hour is the best on the Coast and that at least 25 percent of the shipyard personnel is composed of women and that neither he, his cohorts, or labor in the area would countenance a ten hour shift for women in shipyards."[13] The ten-hour-shift proposal was defeated.

The second approach, discouraging the employment of mothers with young children, was official U.S. government policy until late 1943. The War Manpower Commission issued a statement in August 1942, emphasizing that "the first responsibility of women with young children in war as in peace is to give suitable care to their children" and urging that all other sources of labor be explored before mothers of young children were hired.[14] Government agencies and some industrial personnel departments attempted to implement this policy in the Portland-Vancouver area, urging employers to hire women without children before they considered the employment of mothers. Eleanor Bradley, personnel assistant at Commercial Iron Works, reported in March 1943 that one of her primary concerns was "to get support from the local newspapers in reaching women with young children before they made their original union contact to suggest to them that possibly their most important responsibility is maintaining a normal home situation for their children, rather than turning them over to neighbors, relatives or public facilities."[15] Bradley followed through on her concern by interviewing women who applied for jobs at Commercial and refusing to hire them if they had not made what she considered adequate child-care arrangements.[16]

The Multnomah and Oregon committees on day care, organized in 1942 to coordinate existing child-care programs and applications for federal funds, adopted a similar approach. Both committees made several efforts throughout 1942 to persuade unions and employment services to discourage mothers from working.[17] The Multnomah committee urged that mothers of small children "be taken into industry only when lack of manpower makes it essential and only when such women have first made proper plans for their children."[18] The Oregon Committee took similar care to clarify that their purpose was not to encourage mothers to work but to make sure that the children whose mothers were working received adequate care.[19] The local newspaper also reflected this attitude, even as labor needs intensified in 1943. In an article entitled "Youth on the Loose," *The Oregonian* warned that juvenile delinquency was on the upswing in Portland and quoted a city health officer's disapproving comment that "many mothers apparently prefer $60.00 a week now to good health and behavior for their children later."[20]

Nevertheless, the demand for labor continued to mount, and the strain on community resources made it imperative that local sources of labor be tapped. Women with and without children responded to the call for workers at the shipyards. Unlike managers at Commercial, the management of the Kaiser shipyards did not screen workers to ascertain whether they had made adequate child-care arrangements. They preferred to work with women after they were hired to help them meet their child-care needs. By March 1943 almost half of the fourteen thousand women in the three Kaiser yards were mothers, and about one-third of them had children between the ages of one and six.[21]

As Karen Anderson points out in her study of Baltimore and Seattle, female absenteeism was a clear expression of the burdens of the double day.[22] In early 1943 the national absentee rate was 6.5 percent for women and only 4.5 percent for all workers. In the Portland-Vancouver shipyards, the absentee rate for women was even higher than it was nationally. In October 1943, women's absentee rates were 11.9 percent at Oregon Ship, 11.1 percent at Vancouver, and 13.3 percent at Swan Island, while the corresponding rates for men were 7.32 percent, 9.1 percent, and 9 percent. Absenteeism and turnover quickly became a focus of concern for the production-minded Kaiser management. They had conducted anti-absenteeism campaigns throughout 1942, but absenteeism declined only slightly. Management investigated the problem in a variety of ways and came up with correlations between absenteeism and a range of factors, some of which were quite contradictory. All of the studies showed that women had special problems that were contributing to their higher rates of absenteeism and termination. One study in particular revealed the conflicts involved in adjusting to a workplace that was incompatible with parenting. Women, the study found, often gave family responsibilities as a reason for leaving their jobs but not as a reason for missing work. They did, however, give sickness as the reason for staying home more frequently than men, suggesting that they feared family responsibilities would not be seen as a legitimate excuse.[23]

In the fall of 1943, the personnel department of Oregon Ship conducted a study of one thousand women office workers and welders that, not surprisingly, revealed that women with children lost time more than women without children. More surprisingly, the study also found that welders lost significantly more time than office workers. The study did not specify the shifts that the women were working, so the difference may be explained by the fact that welders were more likely to work swing and night shifts than office workers. Welders were also most likely to work overtime. Production workers often worked six or seven days straight, a schedule that presented additional difficulties for shopping, laundry, and cleaning. The disparity between the Portland-Vancouver figures and the national figures supports the conclusion that production workers had a higher rate of absenteeism than office workers, since the Portland-Vancouver area had a higher percentage of women production workers than most other defense areas.[24]

By late spring 1943, it had become clear to most people in government, industry, and social welfare agencies in the Portland-Vancouver area that discouraging the employment of women with children under the age of fourteen was an unrealistic and inadequate response to the problem, and they began to explore other approaches. There were not enough young women without children to meet the need for labor, and the shipyard management was resistant to hiring older women.

Group Care for Children—the "Last Resort"

The third approach to women's dual responsibilities was to provide facilities that would care for children and reduce the time and anxiety involved in household work. The first effort made in this direction was the hiring of women to act as counselors for women workers. The counselor system, designed to help women solve problems that might contribute to absenteeism and turnover, was recommended by the Women's Bureau and adopted by many defense plants. Counselors helped arrange child care, made doctor and dentist appointments, gave advice about wartime homemaking, and arranged transfers and leaves of absence when necessary.

Kaiser personnel claimed that the counselor system contributed to declining absenteeism rates, but the extent to which counselors eased women's burdens is unclear. The Kaiser management soon recognized that counselors were not enough. They could act as a referral system for available facilities, but there were not enough child-care programs to refer people to. On November 16, 1942, Eleanor Niemi, a counselor at Oregon Ship, reported to the Multnomah County Day Care Committee that thirty women welders would be unable to report to work until they found care for their children. Another personnel officer reported that one mother had to change arrangements eight times before she found adequate care for her children.[25] Similar stories appear in the recollections of the narrators. Nona Pool recalled that "we paid strangers to take care of the kids, and of course we got ripped off plenty on that. I had to furnish their food and furnish their washing and everything, and I found them putting the kids to bed without their supper and then eating the kids' food."[26]

Most of the mothers we interviewed made arrangements within their own families or with neighbors or friends and chose shifts that would most effectively meet their child-care needs. Edna Hopkins, for example, worked swing shift while her husband worked graveyard and "the older ones took care of the younger ones. My husband and I worked opposite shifts so that one of us would be available."[27] Rosa Dickson preferred to work graveyard: "I could put everything away nice, I could slip out and be there at twelve at night and they was all in bed and my husband would be there at twelve."[28] For women without husbands the situation was more difficult. "The way I would get to sleep," explained Audrey Moore, who had come from Louisiana with her son,

I took me a rope and tied it around his waist—because he was very active and he'd like to take off—and . . . tied it in back of him. And he had a little wagon. We had a front and back door where he could go out each door and play and look. So one day I woke up and he was loose. I don't know who let him loose or how he got loose. He was gone. So I had to run all over the place to find him. . . . He had his little wagon and was with some friends around the street. So then I had to get a babysitter.[29]

Two of the shipyard mothers who were interviewed boarded their children with their parents during the war. One of them, Marie Merchant, a black woman from Kentucky, choose this option partly because housing was difficult to find in Portland—doubly difficult for blacks, triply difficult for black people with children.[30] Etta Harvey felt that her child's life, particularly his schooling, would be more stable if he boarded with her parents.[31]

The history of child care during World War II, as several historians have documented, is a confused picture of bureaucratic conflict and ideological ambivalence. Across the country, child-care programs, once they managed to emerge from the complex and confused bureaucratic funding process, were used by far fewer parents than the number who needed them.[32] Karen Anderson, in her study of Detroit, Baltimore, and Seattle, points out that the extent to which child-care facilities were used varied from city to city and argues that parents' use of these programs depended on the quality and convenience of the care offered.[33] As Karen Skold has shown, child-care facilities in the Portland-Vancouver area were used more than in most other communities. Skold has demonstrated that the success of the Portland and Vancouver centers was a result of the interaction between two groups of people, each of which had a different approach to solving the child-care problem. The Kaiser management, concerned about the high absenteeism rates for women, defended the need for child care as a "production problem" and sought solutions in the aggressive manner for which they had become famous. But while the Kaiser approach was responsible for the rapid construction, ample funding, and large scale of the Kaiser child-care operations, Skold suggests that it was the pressure of the day-care committees that was responsible for the high quality of care that inspired the confidence of shipyard parents.[34] The success of the Kaiser centers in turn stimulated the community centers to provide quality care and conduct active publicity campaigns.[35] The result was a child-care program in the Portland-Vancouver area that achieved national acclaim.

The formation of day-care committees was partially stimulated by the allocation in 1942 of federal funds for the assessment of child care needs. Local and state committees were mandated to promote and coordinate programs for the children of working mothers. In the following year, funds became available for the operation of child-care facilities under the Lanham Act, a federal assistance program for war boom communities, and the local committees helped to coordinate the applications. The application process was cumbersome: local agencies had to apply to state agencies which would then forward the applications to Washington.[36]

The local committees which sprang up to organize and coordinate child-care services emerged from the social service and educational communities. In Multnomah County, where the Portland shipyards were located, a subcommittee of the Portland Council of Social Agencies had assessed wartime child-care needs and recommended the formation of an on-going group. The Multnomah County Day Care Committee set up shop in November 1942. Mrs. C. W. Walls, past president of the Oregon Congress of Parents and Teachers, chaired the committee, and she served with nine other representatives of social service agencies, day-care centers, and religious and lay philanthropic organizations.[37]

The child-care group for the state of Oregon began in June 1942 as the Oregon State Advisory Committee on Child Care, Health and Welfare (Oregon Child Care Committee), a thirteen-member advisory committee appointed by the Public Welfare Commission. The committee was reorganized in September 1942 as an affiliate of the Oregon State Defense Council and expanded to include representatives of forty-three social service organizations as well as federal, state and voluntary child-care agencies. It was chaired by Saidie Dunbar, who, as a member of the Women's Advisory Committee of the War Manpower Commission, acted as a liaison between Oregon and Washington, D.C.[38]

These two committees moved cautiously toward the development of child-care facilities, carefully avoiding any action that might be construed as encouraging mothers of young children to work. Elizabeth Goddard, secretary of Multnomah County Day Care Committee, remembered that the "committee was called all sorts of names by the conservative people – that we were forcing women out of the home. And that we were doing terrible things to children."[39] Some members also feared that the committees would be used as the means by which dictatorial government agencies would intervene in the activities of private programs. The representatives from Catholic Charities and

Volunteers of America, for example, insisted that the Oregon committee's initial statement make it clear that it had no intention of taking over private child-care agencies.[40]

The day-care committees began their work by assessing needs and meeting with various people involved with the child-care problem. In August 1942, the nine full-time preschool centers in the Multnomah County area were practically full and there was increasing demand for extended day programs for school-age children. The Oregon Child Care Committee had taken the position early in its existence that group care should be developed in the school system as part of the educational program. Members of the Portland School Board, however, did not believe that mothers of young children should be working and were reluctant to take responsibility for administering a preschool program. After considerable pressure from the day-care committees, the school board voted unanimously to apply for federal funding, but hastened to explain that "the nursery program is not construed as an invitation to mothers of small children to go to work in war plants."[41]

By the spring of 1943 there were ten preschool centers in Portland and two in Vancouver, but they were not consistently operating at capacity. Several features of the centers may have limited their use. Because they were located in the community, they often presented transportation difficulties; none were open twenty-four hours a day, which meant they were not useful for either swing- or night-shift mothers; and some did not open early enough to accommodate day-shift mothers. Only three centers admitted children under the age of two.[42]

"The Factory of the Future"

The Kaiser management had said in 1942 that it would prefer that the community develop child-care facilities, but by spring of 1943 as increasing numbers of mothers joined the shipyard work force, Kaiser became impatient with the pace of the community day-care programs. At Oregon Ship alone, 830 mothers of pre school age children were on the job in March, 1943. In May Henry Kaiser announced plans to construct three nurseries, one at each of the shipyards. Each nursery was expected to have a capacity of 450 children. Kaiser had applied for funding from the U.S. Maritime Commission, arguing that the child-care centers were necessary to expedite production. He was therefore able to bypass the local day-care committees and avoid the complicated procedure involved in applying for Lanham Act funds.[43] Early in June Kaiser and his two sons brought the child-care center plans to Eleanor Roosevelt who wrote to Admiral Emory Scott Land, chairman of the Maritime Commission, urging him to give the Kaisers "the go-ahead signal." Eleanor Roosevelt did not share the belief of the War Manpower Commission and the majority of the members of the local day-care committees that women with young children should not be working. "I have long known," she wrote, "that the only way we could possible [sic] get the women that we need to take jobs was to provide them with community services. . . . If the shipbuilding companies will recognize this fact, that it is a part of being able to do their jobs to render these services, it may spread to other industries and will help enormously in war production."[44]

In this case, however, the problem lay not with the shipbuilding company but with the local day-care committees. The day-care committees of Multnomah County, Vancouver, and the State of Oregon all opposed the construction of the Kaiser child-care centers and used a variety of methods to thwart Kaiser's plans. Their opposition was shared by the U.S. Office of Education and the U.S. Children's Bureau, both of which sent representatives to the area in May to study the matter. The Women's Advisory Committee of the War Manpower Commission also opposed the construction of the centers, as did the Oregon State Medical Society. Letters were sent, reports were prepared, and a new interstate committee was formed to mobilize opposition to the Kaiser plan.[45]

The day-care committee members and their supporters presented a variety of arguments against the construction of the centers. They believed that day-care centers should be located in neighborhoods rather than at the workplace; they feared the spread of diseases in group care on the scale that Kaiser contemplated; they worried about the vulnerability of centers located at shipyards that might be likely targets of enemy bombings. Opponents of the Kaiser plan also contended that the existing facilities were underused, and were concerned that the shipyard centers would duplicate and perhaps undermine the neighborhood and housing project centers. Finally, they maintained that child-care centers should be run not by industry but by educational institutions that understood the needs of young children.[46] "Child care services," according to Hazel Fredericksen of the Children's Bureau," should not be isolated from other child health, educational, recreational and social services for children."[47]

Underlying these arguments were two distinct but related attitudes: a continued reluctance to encourage mothers of young children to work outside the home, and a deep suspicion of industrial involvement in the family life of workers. "Involvement of the employer in the care of employees' children," argued Hazel Fredericksen, "violates the sound principle of an impersonal objective approach to industrial problems for both employer and employee."[48] Day-care committee members and Children's Bureau staff feared that Kaiser would disregard the welfare of children in his driving desire to recruit labor for his shipyards and that once nurseries were established under the aegis of industry, decisions would be made based on the needs of industry rather than the needs of children. For example, Saidie Dunbar, outraged by a rumor that the Kaiser centers included plans for infant care, wrote to Jerold Owen of the Oregon Defense Council, "None of us believe that the manpower shortage actually demands the services of mothers of six-month-old babies."[49] An exchange between Edgar Kaiser and Mrs. William Keltzer, a day-care committee member, at a meeting of the state committee on August 4, 1943, further revealed this tension. Keltzer expressed concern about the vulnerability of the centers to air-raid attacks and suggested that they be built somewhere else. Kaiser responded that the committee did not seem to understand the magnitude of the problem, which, he predicted, would intensify as more women were hired. He suggested that since most women at the Kaiser yards preferred child care at their place of work, it would be democratic to respect their wishes. In response Keltzer suggested that the parents' judgment is not always in the best interest of the child and cited child labor as an example of this phenomenon, conjuring up an image of industry ruthlessly exploiting the needs of working people.[50]

Because they believed that young children were best off being cared for by mothers at home, day-care committee members saw Kaiser's willingness to provide care for young children as an example of his subordination of the needs of young children to those of the shipyards. They reminded him that the War Manpower Commission discouraged the employment of women whose children were under fourteen and urged him to explore more fully the employment of more women without children. It was apparent that the committee was opposed not only to the kind of care Kaiser was planning to offer but to the possibility that such care would encourage mothers to work.[51]

In fact Henry Kaiser and his son Edgar did, at least in their public wartime stance, see the question of women workers and their future in industry differently from most of the members of the day-care committees. In an interview in *The New York Times* in October 1943, Henry Kaiser argued that "factories should be equipped with child-care centers, health clinics, shopping centers, food dispensers, banking facilities, dry cleaning shops, recreation centers, comfortable lockers and rest rooms." Kaiser claimed that he saw these services not merely as emergency measures but as features of what he called "the factory of the future."[52]

Kaiser proceeded with the construction of two of the child-care centers without the approval of the day-care committees, but dropped his plans for a center at the Vancouver shipyard. The Vancouver Public Schools and the Clark County Child Care Committee were moving more quickly towards the construction of Lanham-funded child-care centers. Four centers were in operation and plans for seven more housing project centers were under way. The Interstate and Washington day-care committees convinced the Kaiser management that facilities were adequate in the Vancouver area, and Edgar Kaiser made a public statement explaining "that the greater part of the Vancouver Yard employees live in a concentrated community in the housing areas, which makes the neighborhood child-care centers practical. By contrast Oregon Ship and Swan Island workers are spread throughout Portland and its suburbs."[53]

Recognizing that they could not prevent Kaiser from building the two Portland centers, the Multnomah County Day Care Committee agreed to work with the Kaiser management. They played a significant role in inspiring the Kaiser management to develop not only the biggest but the best child-care center in the country.[54] The Kaisers knew nothing about early childhood education and originally planned to use the same pool of job applicants to staff the child-care centers that they were using to hire welders. Once convinced that they needed professionals, however, they committed themselves to securing the best-qualified staff in the country.

Service to Children and Families

Edgar Kaiser took an important step toward regaining the trust of the social work and education professionals by asking the U.S. Office of Education, the central administrator of the Lanham Act nurseries, and the Children's Bureau to recommend an administrator for the new centers. At the suggestion of all three agencies, he approached Lois Meek Stolz, former director of the Child Development Institute at Columbia University Teachers College. Stolz was impressed by the Kaisers' openness and willingness to learn and, while she was unable to leave her job and family in San Francisco, she was so intrigued by the scale of the project and the resources available that she agreed to serve as consultant and overall director, visiting the centers for one week each month. Her former student, James Hymes, was appointed on-site manager. James Hymes had formerly directed the Hessian Hills School in Croton on Hudson, New York, and was well known as an advocate of progressive education. Released from his job at the Pentagon by a well-placed phone call from Edgar Kaiser, Hymes quickly adapted to the Kaiser style of work, sent two-page telegrams to all the nursery school people he knew, and recruited a highly trained child-care staff and the top child nutritionist in the country.[55]

For a brief moment in history, the competitive principles of the marketplace were applied to the historically underfunded profession of early childhood education. An interview with Lois Stolz, conducted by James Hymes, in which the two tell the story of the centers abounds with examples of this, such as the recollection of Kaiser expediters "riding herd on play equipment." But the most stunning illustration is the story of the salary scale ($60 per week for head teachers, $43 for assistant teachers).

> When I first discussed salaries with Edgar Kaiser I proposed that we pay the same wage that teachers were getting in the Lanham Act war nurseries, because I didn't want us to compete. I told Mr. Kaiser the figure and he almost exploded. "You can't pay college graduates that! You won't hold them a week. All the administrative offices in the yards will steal them away from you." So we had to *up* our salary scale and, of course, we didn't fight the idea.[56]

James Hymes and most of the people he recruited were committed to progressive education. They believed that children should be encouraged to be independent and that nursery schools should nurture children's spirit of adventure and inquiry. They now found they had the resources to put these ideas fully into practice: child-sized furniture and bathroom fixtures, straight-edged plates so that "the beginning feeder could catch his food and succeed in feeding himself," bibs that children could put on by themselves, and play equipment designed to generate "richness and challenge" – all funded by the Maritime Commission. Sometimes the supplies and materials were requisitioned from manufacturers and speeded across the country by Kaiser expediters, and sometimes they were custom-made by local people with a "Kaiser expediter constantly on the phone, checking, reminding, nagging."[57]

The Kaiser Child Service Centers were housed not in church basements or unused elementary school space, but in two buildings specifically designed to meet the needs of young children. The fifteen class-

The 18-month-olds' room at the Kaiser Child Service Center.
Courtesy of the Oregon Historical Society, negative #60695.

rooms, each equipped for twenty-five children, were arranged like the spokes of a wheel surrounding playground space and a wading pool. A covered area in each playground allowed children to play outside on the rainy days that are a constant feature of Portland weather from November to May.[58]

The staff of the Kaiser Center anticipated the opening of the center with excitement and, aware of the national significance of their project, were committed to publicizing it as widely as possible. Lois Stolz described the centers in an article in *The New York Times Magazine*, concluding "the staff is preparing to make Portland the focal point of the nation in the care of working mothers of preschool children."[59]

The Kaiser Child Service Centers impressed educators around the world with the scale, variety and quality of their program. The two centers were open twenty-four hours a day, serving all three shipyard shifts, and were expected to serve over 1,000 children each. The staff members of the child-care centers were committed to combining the best that the nursery school tradition had to offer with a program flexible enough to meet the needs of working mothers. Since this was an experiment for most early childhood educators they constantly reassessed needs and developed new programs – one of the most impressive features of the Kaiser centers. The inclusion of the word *Service* in the name of the new centers conveys one of their most revolutionary features. The staff conceived of centers as a resource for working parents and their children, of which child care was one facet. "A mother working in a shipyard," wrote Miriam Lowenberg, the chief nutritionist, "with any problem relating to children may find here a place where she may seek help."[60]

The ideological ambivalence that prevented many wartime institutions from responding adequately to the needs of wage-earning mothers was conspicuously absent at the Kaiser Centers. Staff members were determined that "no peace-time precept, no *a priori* rule must stand in the way of service to children, to families."[61] The staff of the child service centers were attracted to the project of providing high-quality child care for children of working mothers and were therefore committed to responding flexibly to the needs of children and parents. They addressed the special needs of swing-shift children, whose sleep was disrupted by parents leaving work; they set up a mending service where parents could bring torn clothing; produced many educational materials for parents about the physical and emotional needs of children, and provided extended care for parents who needed to attend a union meeting or go shopping. They established an infirmary where mildly ill children could be isolated from others and cared for by nurses without requiring their mothers to miss work. They organized immunization clinics, a drop-in service

Classroom at the Kaiser Child Service Center. *Courtesy of the Oregon Historical Society, negative #80378.*

Playground at the Kaiser Child Service Center with wading pool in the center. *Courtesy of the Oregon Historical Society, negative #80379.*

Covered play area at the Kaiser Child Service Center. *Courtesy of the Oregon Historical Society, negative #80377.*

where parents could bring their children in emergencies, and summer-long and after-school programs for six- and seven-year-olds. Borrowing an idea from England, the centers prepared take-out meals that parents could pick up when they called for their children at the end of the shifts.[62]

The ample resources of the Kaiser Child Service Centers were made possible by the Maritime Commission. The commission built the buildings and paid for the initial equipment. Parents paid $5.00 for a six-day week and $3.75 for each additional child, but this contributed less than one-third the operating cost.[63] All costs above that covered by parents' fees were paid by Kaiser corporation and passed on to the Maritime Commission as part of the shipbuilding contract. James Hymes, in his final report on the centers, emphasized the importance of this federal subsidy and commented, "All education is deficit-producing, and Child Service Centers are no exception. The greater the number of children served, the greater the deficit."[64]

The Kaiser Child Service Centers quickly gained a national reputation among people concerned with the employment of women as

The Infirmary at the Kaiser Child Service Center. *Courtesy of the Oregon Historical Society, negative #80273.*

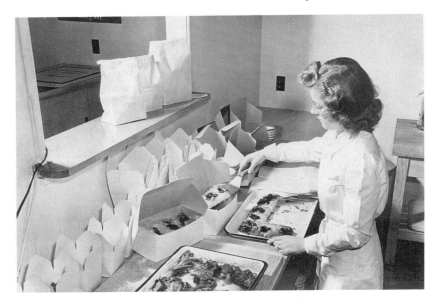

Take home food at the Kaiser Child Service Center. *Courtesy of the Oregon Historical Society, negative #80373.*

well as early childhood educators. "I have never seen anything so remarkable," wrote Mary Alice Webb after her Portland visit in 1944. "They are open 24 hours per day and are so advanced they actually beggar description."[65] Kaiser received an award from *Parents Magazine* for the high quality of the child-care centers, and sixteen articles appeared in professional journals describing the centers' contribution to early childhood education.[66]

Even the recalcitrant members of the local day-care committees were won over by the staff of the Kaiser Child Service Centers. Kaiser Center staff members joined the Multnomah County committee and contributed a great deal to the child-care community. They organized monthly symposia to which they often invited experts from out of town, helped to found the Oregon Association of Nursery Educators, and were generous about sharing their expertise and resources.[67] The social workers and educators on the day-care committees found many of their previous assumptions about children challenged by the Kaiser Child Service Centers. "We learned an awful lot from the Kaiser nurseries," reflected Elizabeth Goddard. "Some of these things that we were sure were going to happen didn't happen at all."[68] Occasional echoes of the early opposition to industrial child care reappeared in the committee deliberations, but in general committee members appreciated the contributions of the centers.[69]

The Kaiser centers also served to stimulate community efforts to provide child-care services. The Vancouver Public Schools took responsibility for group care for working mothers in April 1943 and, working closely with the Clark County Committee on Day Care, utilized both Lanham Act and state funds to develop a child-care program. By April 1944, there were eight child-care centers in Vancouver serving 775 children, and of the 10,000 attending Vancouver public schools, 3,000 were involved in extended-day programs. All but one of the Vancouver elementary schools went on double shift in the beginning of 1943 as a result of the influx of over 3,000 children into the community. As a result, extended-day programs were urgently needed.[70] In Portland in February 1944, there were twenty nurseries operating in housing projects and neighborhoods serving an average of 841 children a day. The Portland Public Schools, in addition to running eleven of these centers, also operated six extended-day programs.[71]

The Use of Child-Care Centers

The experience of the Portland-Vancouver area offers useful insights into the puzzling question of the underutilization of child-care facilities during the war. Contemporary observers cited the following reasons that child-care centers across the country operated under capacity: centers were inadequately publicized; they were not located in convenient locations; and parents were reluctant to leave children with people they didn't know, lacked confidence in the quality of care the centers provided, and feared the spread of contagious disease in large groups of children.[72] Historians have also suggested that parents were resistant to institutional child care because they associated group care with welfare and they feared that their children would not get individual attention.[73]

Augusta Clawson, who was at Swan Island shortly before the Kaiser Child Service Centers opened, encountered suspicion of group child care among the women she worked with. "I was surprised to observe," she reported, "that no one took to the nursery idea at first."

"I don't want my kid playing with just anybody's kid," said one woman. "My Dickie's fussy about eating. I have to watch his food," another protested. But when it was made clear that the nursery would be well staffed with a doctor and nurses, that the children would receive excellent care and that it was not a "charity thing" their interest picked up.[74]

A close examination of the Portland and Vancouver experience demonstrates that the effect of negative attitudes toward group child care diminished with improved service, publicity, and education. All centers were underused when they first opened, but attendance increased over time at most facilities. Attendance at the programs operated by the public schools in Portland and Vancouver fluctuated dramatically. The ambivalence of the Portland public school board about running the program and the bureaucratic confusion of the federal grant program created constant uncertainty about the centers. For example, in August 1943, the $50,000 that had been allotted by the federal government for preschool programs was used up. Although the school board had applied for more money for the preschool and school-age programs, no action had been taken on the application. An article in *The Oregonian* of August 21 announced that eleven nursery schools and thirty summer programs for school-age children were to be closed. "Board Chairman Robert Ormond Case pointed out that the problem of providing daycare for children of working mothers was 'wished' on the board by social and governmental agencies and the board has 'reluctantly' agreed to sponsor the program only if the federal works agency would provide the funds!"[75] The following day it was announced that the centers were to stay open after all. The Federal Works Administration representatives explained that the money had been available for some time but the requisition had only been received five days before.[76] Had the centers closed, the parents of 750 children would have had to find alternative child-care arrangements. Such incidents must certainly have impaired the trust of working parents, who needed arrangements they could depend on.

Whatever uneasiness parents felt about child-care centers must have been magnified for black parents, who encountered racial discrimination in the community and the workplace. Only one center in Portland attracted substantial numbers of black children – The Blessed Martin Day Nursery. Located in the black community and run by the Society of St. Vincent De Paul, Blessed Martin was full or above its twenty-eight-child capacity throughout the war.[77] Most child-care centers were run by white staff and inevitably reflected the racism of the community. The Kaiser Child Service centers were no exception. Of 450 parents whose children were enrolled at the two centers in 1943, only three were black, and the numbers never increased much.[78] While Virginia Lemire, Coordinator of Counseling Services at the

Kaiser Yards, claimed black parents had made previous arrangements and therefore didn't need the centers, Lois Stolz recognized the apprehensiveness of black parents about white institutions.

> Looking back on it the fault was in large part ours. We had no black staff members. And we learned, near the end that our buildings looked so grandiose to black mothers. At that time they couldn't quite believe the Centers were for their children too. And some, we learned, were afraid that our white teachers would hit their youngsters.[77]

Despite the efforts of the staff, the racial tensions of the community seeped into the child service centers, preventing them from being a comfortable place for black children. A nurse at the Kaiser Centers remembered the day a black child came to the center for the first time.

> Well, that day everything was fine because she came after the rest of the group was started. Then that evening here comes the parents to pick up their children and they see this colored girl. Well they just hit the ceiling. And after that, then there was a little trouble among the children. Then they all didn't accept her quite as well as they had the first day.[80]

The use of child-care facilities in both Vancouver and Portland increased steadily throughout the war. In the fall of 1944 Portland was allotted the full $157,351 that the school board had requested to operate its eleven nursery schools and six extended-day programs. Vancouver, with a combination of state and federal funding, was operating eight nursery schools in the city of Vancouver and five at housing projects in outlying areas. Enrollment continued to increase during 1944 and 1945. In Vancouver, 557 children were enrolled in child-care programs in January 1944, and by the following January 936 children were enrolled.[81]

The most dramatic increases were at the Kaiser centers, where enrollment tripled. The original plan to care for over 1,000 children at each center was revised through practice, and capacity was defined at 350 children for each center. The adjusted definition of capacity reflected a variety of staffing and space factors, the most important of which was that day shift and swing shift overlapped, rendering only half the classrooms available. When the two centers opened in November 1943, only 68 children registered at Swan Island and 79 at Oregon Ship, demonstrating the need for more publicity and education.

The reputation of child care centers improved with time and effort. Shipyard mothers needed to know not only that the centers were safe environments but that there were positive advantages to sending their children there. Edna Hopkins, for example, left Mona, her two-year-old with her older sisters most of the time even though she was convinced that the child care center in Vanport was "clean and neat" and that "they did take good care of them." She was, however, uncertain that Mona's invidual needs would be met and therefore saw a family solution as preferable. Hopkins sent Mona to the Vanport Center for a little while, but

> she didn't like it because she was sort of an independent little girl, I guess, and the first day she went they made her wear somebody's else's shoes and she knew they weren't her shoes. . . . She said, "These aren't my shoes," but the girl didn't pay any attention to her. And she came home with the wrong shoes on, and I took her back and got her shoes and the girl said, "She said they weren't her shoes." . . . I said, "The next time, believe her, because she knows her shoes." She just got sort of off on the wrong foot like that. And she was used to being around older children. . . . She said the kids cried a lot and that bothered her. She didn't really enjoy that. But she didn't have to go too often.[82]

The staff of the Kaiser Child Service Centers recognized the need to demonstrate to parents that the difficulties involved in group care for children were offset by the benefits.[83] The Centers conducted daily tours through the centers, wrote articles for the newspapers, and produced pamphlets explaining the centers' services.

By March 1944 the two Kaiser centers together served 605 children. Attendance increased even more during the summer when programs for young school-age children were added, reaching a peak in the first week of September with 1,005 children. The centers operated under capacity most of the time but that was, to a large extent, because of the underuse of graveyard-shift care, which most parents found inconvenient. During one month in the summer of 1944, for example, 465 children were cared for at the two centers during the day shift. Karen Skold has shown that the percentage of children who used the two Kaiser yards was significantly higher than contemporary estimates in most other war boom communities. (Five percent of the children of working mothers in a national survey conducted by the Women's Bureau were in child-care centers, while 22 percent of the preschool children of shipyard mothers at the Kaiser yards used the centers.) Attendance at the centers declined in the fall of 1944 as increasing numbers of women shipyard workers were laid off.[84]

The experience of the summer programs for school-age children run by the Portland school boards affords another illustration of the importance of education and publicity. In June 1943, six of the vacation-care programs closed for lack of attendance. Attendance at programs that remained open, however, increased from 340 to 900 within one week.[85] The following fall the summer programs opened with a warning that if attendance dropped below 15 at any one center for any one week, the center would close. All centers remained open throughout the summer since attendance was good, ranging from 20 to 80 at each school and totalling 800. The school with the highest enrollment was Chapman, whose principal directed the summer-school program and made information about the center more readily available than at other schools.[86]

As the above discussion demonstrates, the use of wartime child-care programs in the Portland-Vancouver area increased as centers became better known, as parents became more confident about the quality of care, and as programs became more responsive to the varied needs of the community. Location seemed to be an important factor in the success of preschool facilities. Having to make an extra trip to take a child to a center complicated an already long and complex day. Nell Conley's life, for example, was greatly simplified by the opening of the Oregon Ship Child Service Center. "For the first six months or so I got up at 5:30 in the morning, bundled my four-year child into heavy clothes, took her with two bus transfers to the home of a woman who was taking care of three or four other shipyard mothers' children, then caught the Fessenden bus to the shipyard."[87] Centers located in housing projects, however, were particularly useful for swing-shift mothers. A teacher at the University Homes child-care center, which served three shifts, reported that the center filled up immediately and "always had a waiting list."[88] Swing shift workers could bring their children in the afternoon, leave them there throughout the night, and pick them up the next morning after both had had a night's sleep.

The popularity of child-care centers grew despite the instability of many programs and the lack of ideological support for the idea of group care. Both the community and the workplace child-care programs in Portland and Vancouver achieved national acclaim. "Oregon," wrote Jerold Owen to Saidie Dunbar at the end of 1943, "is recognized nationally as having a child-care program second to none."[89] Lillian Herstein, the director of the labor relations division of the War Production League, declared the Vancouver program "tops in the nation."[90]

In the spring of 1944, James Hymes wrote of

the hope each teacher has that here in Portland ground is being broken for a vast postwar development in nursery education. There is the vision that perhaps the Kaiser answer to a wartime problem can show the way to a country's answer to similar peacetime needs. This experiment in cooperation may lead other industries, other communities, other government agencies, other parents to provide similar facilities.[91]

The story of the Kaiser centers and the other facilities it helped to inspire *could have* represented a watershed in the history of women workers and the history of child care. The child-service centers demonstrated to skeptical observers that sound preschool education could take place in an industrial setting and that children did not become maladjusted as a result of group care. But after the war the precedent set by the Kaiser child service centers was forgotten. The postwar emphasis on the primacy of women's domestic roles precluded serious consideration of child care. Even Henry Kaiser forgot the bold predictions he had made in the interview of October 1943. Although the percentage of women in the work force who had preschool-age children returned to its wartime level by 1950, the Kaiser experiments remained buried until the early 1970s, when the emergence of feminism stimulated a reconsideration of social solutions for the problems of working mothers.[92]

4 ☆ "WHAT WILL HAPPEN WHEN THE BOYS COME HOME?"

As the previous chapters have demonstrated, attitudes about women war workers were complex. While the dominant messages emphasized the immutability of the traditional division of labor at home and the ephemeral nature of changes in the workplace, glimmers of vision and possibility such as the Kaiser Child Service Centers seemed to promise enduring transformation in women's position in the home and the workplace. In addition to the implicit messages of wartime society and culture about the postwar role of women wage earners, there was an outpouring of speculation, debate, and concern about what would happen to women workers "when the boys came home."[1] Because postwar culture was dominated by conservative ideas about women, any wartime attempts to safeguard women's rights in the industrial work force quickly became buried under the emerging myth that women workers happily receded into domesticity. It is important, however, to recover what E. P. Thompson has called the "blind alleys, the lost causes and the losers themselves," for, as Ferdinand Braudel has noted, such drowned possibilities, "have at every moment affected the final outcome."[2]

The National Picture

A survey of major national periodicals and the documents of agencies concerned with the employment of working women makes it clear that there was no cultural consensus about the postwar fate of women workers. The number of articles devoted to speculation about the subject indicates that it was not universally assumed that women would leave either the paid work force or the industrial work force after the war. The *Ladies' Home Journal* asked in 1944 whether the new women workers will "be willing, when the war is over, to return quietly to the dishpan, handing back to the returning hero his job and his pay envelope?"[3] The nation was deeply divided on the answer. "The last war," observed Harry Truman in August 1943, when he was chairing the Senate War Investigating Committee, "put the women into offices and they never left them. This war has put them into factories. Let no one imagine that women will permit themselves to be shunted out of these jobs which they have demonstrated so well their capacity to do."[4] On the other hand, a study done by the Brookings Institution in 1943 reported that the women who had been working during the war would "of course be among the first to be demobilized when the war ends. It seems unlikely that many of these women will wish to remain permanently in the labor force.... In any case it would be difficult to argue that provision of permanent employment for this group is a paramount national obligation."[5]

There was, however, a constellation of groups, individual, government agencies, and journals that argued this position vociferously. It included groups that were part of what Cynthia Harrison has called "the Women's Bureau Coalition," as well as organizations that supported the Equal Rights Amendment.[6] These groups disagreed about strategies, and there were divisions within some of the groups, but they were united in their defense of the rights of women workers.

While as some historians have noted, the debate on the position of women during the war did not address basic issues about the sexual division of labor, women's groups did raise questions about women in the work force.[7] They may have been a minority, they may have been ignored by most people in power, and they may have backed away from the most radical implications of their questions, but they did ask them. In a variety of forums they publicly argued that women's jobs deserved as much protection as men's and that women did not or should not always prefer domestic roles. They questioned "any easy assumption" that large numbers of women would "return to their homes" after the war, urged that postwar employment policy be based on the principle of "complete equality for men and women," and suggested shortening hours and lengthening vacations to maintain enough jobs for all, including women.[8] They submitted resolutions to the War Manpower Commission designed to ensure equal treatment of women in the reconversion period and lobbied state by state for equal pay laws, which they believed would prevent the return to the "cycle of cheapness" that had characterized women's roles in the prewar work force.[9] "Women," argued Theresa Wolfson, "cannot be cast aside like an old glove. To be sure, many working women will be glad to go back to their homes and their aprons. The choice, however, will be made by them as adult mature members of society – not *for* them."[10]

Wolfson's emphasis on choice was not typical of the arguments or predictions of the wartime advocates of women workers. In general they stressed women workers' *need* to continue in the work force and avoided confronting traditional assumptions about the sexual division in the family. They eschewed what they called "a narrowly feminist view," which saw women as individuals, in favor of one which emphasized their roles and functions in the family and the community. Contending that women wage earners were working because they needed to, not because they wanted to, was a strategy intended to counter the prevailing assumption that women worked for "pin money" and therefore did not need equal treatment in the work force. The argument served a dual purpose: challenging the trivialization of women's waged work and allaying the fear that the employment of women was a repudiation of family roles.[11]

Similarly, the constellation of women's groups led by the Women's Bureau was not prepared to argue that women should have access to all jobs. They advocated expansion of the number of jobs open to women based on women's wartime record, but they defined women as different, as having a "peculiar contribution to make."[12] The defensive posture of these arguments demonstrates that the atmosphere of the wartime period was not friendly to feminist ideas. Judith Sealander observes that the Women's Bureau and its allies were "torn between demands for equal pay and equal opportunity for women workers and rhetorical commitments to traditional views of the family and women's roles. They were Outsiders as Insiders, fence sitters. Their wartime complaints usually met silence."[13]

The groups and individuals engaged in planning and advocacy for women wage earners understood, through extensive study and research, that the number of women in the work force would continue to increase in the postwar world, despite the popular image of a massive retreat of women from the work force. They battled mightily against this misconception, publicizing their studies where they could, but most of their findings remained buried in the *Monthly Labor Review* and internal newsletters and bulletins. The Women's Bureau study that received the most attention drew on a survey of women workers about their postwar plans. The survey was conducted in 1944 and 1945 but was not published until 1946, at which point excerpts found their way into newspapers and magazines across the country. The study revealed that three-quarters of the women interviewed in ten production areas wanted to continue working for wages and that 86 percent of those women wanted to remain in the same occupational group in which they were employed during the war. The study also demonstrated that the postwar demand for women workers was likely to be far greater in the trade and service sector than in the manufacturing industries, where most of the women production workers wanted to remain.[14]

The women's groups recognized the danger. They understood that women would be pushed into the major "woman-employing" industries at low pay by discriminatory practices on the part of both labor and management. They also understood that women workers would continue to be viewed with suspicion by male workers if they were willing to accept low wages, citing World War I and its aftermath as evidence of this dynamic. They therefore worked simultaneously to safeguard women's rights in male-dominated industries while trying to upgrade the conditions in women-employing industries. They also urged employment services to treat women workers equally and offer them the training necessary to adapt their wartime skills to peacetime use.[15]

All of these efforts to protect the position of women in the postwar labor market had little impact on postwar planning. Despite the efforts of women's groups, few women were appointed to postwar planning committees in government, industry, or labor, and those few were too isolated to have any significant impact.[16] As the end of the war approached, articles urging women to retire from the work force or predicting that women would do so willingly appeared with increasing frequency in newspapers and magazines. They expressed a range of attitudes, including unabashed calls for the return to a mythical age of domestic bliss in which

> Mrs. Jones will make the bed – the chore that bored us worst of all – and we'll find the house clean and lighted when we get home at night. The table will be set in shining array for supper! We'll forget this catch-as-catch-can, red-and-blue point three-shift way of living.[17]

The Ladies Home Journal championed a similar image of domestic bliss but did endorse equal pay for equal work. Supporting the right of self-supporting women to postwar jobs, it quoted a San Diego woman who complained that "a single woman is as disabled as a soldier." Married women, however, who had comprised the largest number of new workers and represented a steadily increasing proportion of the female work force, received no such support. *The Journal* conducted its own survey of women workers and, although over half the women in the survey reported that they did not plan to stop working after the war, *The Journal* concluded that, "women want marriage and homemaking, not factory jobs; that they work in industry only because they have to or for an emergency and that they want man's wages as long as they do man's work."[18] In response to the disconcerting finding that 79 percent of the women in the survey reported that they enjoyed working more than staying at home, *The Journal* concluded that women believed that "Jobs are more enjoyable, but homes are more important."[19]

Postwar Worries in the Portland-Vancouver Area

Regional economic conditions heavily influenced wartime attitudes toward women's postwar position in the labor force. In the West anxiety about the future was acute since the wartime boom had attracted thousands of workers to cities that had little or no industry before the war. The uncertain future of the dominant industry heightened anxiety in the Portland-Vancouver area. (In some people's eyes the future of the area rested with one man – Henry Kaiser.) In 1940, less than 20 percent of the labor force in Portland had been industrially employed; by 1944, 92 percent of the total labor force was engaged in shipbuilding.[20] Of the 137,000 men and women working in war industries in Portland at the end of 1943, 45,000 had been recruited from other jobs in the area, 25,000 (mostly women) had not been working before the war, and 67,000 had migrated from other parts of the country.[21] The shipbuilding boom in Portland, commented *Fortune*, had "made this once comfortable and complacent city perhaps the most uncomfortable and least self-satisfied along the entire coast."[22]

Both Vancouver and Portland began preparing for their postwar dilemmas in 1943, when they formed postwar planning committees. The mayor of Portland appointed a forty-seven-member group to "study and recommend action on the problems of postwar planning for employment and healthy urban growth."[33] The composition of the Portland Area Postwar Development Committee (PAPDC), like that of national planning committees, did not augur well for women, blacks, or workers. Twenty-five of the committee's members were businessmen, nine were public officials, one represented labor, and the remainder were professionals, journalists, educators, and religious leaders. The committee was entirely white and entirely male.[24] According to E. Kimbark MacColl, the PAPDC was dominated by the banks and utilities, a combination, MacColl notes, not unusual in Portland's history.[25] Although the Oregon Federation of Women's Clubs had passed a resolution in 1942 protesting the "fact that women are not receiving justifiable recognition on policy committees" on a national level, there is no record of local efforts to include women in the Portland Committee.[26]

The all-male planning committee stands in sharp contrast to the high level of women's involvement in the state and city volunteer committees that addressed wartime problems such as civil defense, child care, rationing, and blood and war bond drives. The women's pages of *The Oregonian* carried detailed accounts of women's volunteer activities and conferences on the problems of the wartime community and awarded weekly citations to women leaders.[27] There was female leadership available, but it was used selectively.

The massive influx of workers into the Portland-Vancouver area stimulated speculations about postwar economic conditions everywhere in the community. The postwar future of the shipbuilding industry did not look bright, since it depended on the wartime needs of the U.S. Maritime Commission, but throughout 1944 government and industry exerted considerable energy attempting to prevent workers from acting on this realization. Thousands of workers were leaving the shipyards in search of jobs that offered more stability. The Maritime Commission assured workers that while the shipbuilding boom might fade, there would be enough demand for ship repair, improvement, and conversion to "assure yards in this area of a permanent place in America's postwar shipbuilding program."[28] While avoiding promises of postwar jobs, Edgar Kaiser pleaded with workers not to "sell the Northwest short" and to remain in Portland and Vancouver, the "best places in the nation to work. . . . There will be a tremendous repair load when the war is over," he told Swan Island workers in May 1944. "Troop ships will have to be converted when the boys are brought back and if we can do it cheaper here we will do the work."[29] Governor Langlie of Washington joined the chorus in August, assuring citizens that Washington had the "resources to meet the problems in the post-war years."[30]

But when the purpose of the predictions was to estimate the need for government aid to unemployed workers after the war, a more sober tone prevailed. By July 1944 the Oregon Unemployment Compensation Commission was warning that "of the 110,000 individuals who will have been added since 1940 by firms engaged in shipbuilding or allied work, it does not seem unreasonable to assume that all but 1,000 will have to seek work in other industries.[31] Hope for avoiding massive unemployment after the war lay outside the shipbuilding industry – in the development of new industry, the underwriting of public works projects, or a boom in the construction of private homes. The only other source of redemption for the Portland employment picture was the possibility that many of the newcomers to the area would leave and *The Christian Science Monitor* reported that Portland was in fact asking its workers to return to their prewar homes when the war was over.[32] Simmering tensions between new and old residents rose to the surface as the end of the war approached.[33]

The Portland Area Postwar Development Committee (PAPDC) adopted a step-by-step approach to solving postwar problems and began by gathering information about the plans of both workers and industry. On the basis of this information, it planned to "determine the employment and income, taking into consideration skills and transferability from one industry or occupation to another, stability of certain industries and what training is to be given new workers."[34] Understanding the importance of developing new sources of employment in the Portland area, the PAPDC joined with several other Portland agencies in November 1943 to bring New York City parks commissioner Robert Moses to the area to develop a postwar public works program. Since Moses and his staff were only in Portland for a short time, they drew heavily upon research and planning done by the PAPDC before their arrival.[35]

The report of the Moses Committee, *Portland Improvement*, which recommended a series of expensive public works projects, did not relieve apprehensions about the postwar employment picture.[36] It warned that even under optimal conditions jobs for the 137,000 workers could probably not be found. According to the report, uncertainty about the plans of workers who had come to Portland for war jobs made predictions about the future difficult, but no such hesitance inhibited the committee's ability to predict the behavior of the women workers. In calculating the number of people who would need jobs when the war ended, it subtracted the 25,000 workers who were "working in war plants who did not work before" on the assumption that they would "become readjusted to peacetime habits."[37]

According to *Portland Improvement*, Portland could expect to experience an economic slump after the war ended, although "retirement of most of the women workers will help." But the Moses Committee warned that "there will be a period of unemployment even if all women in industry retire gracefully, if at least half of the newcomers go back to their homes or elsewhere and if business revives and expands in answer to insistent unsatisfied consumer demands."[38] Like postwar planners throughout the country, the Moses Committee blithely ignored the reports of the Women's Bureau that most women employed in defense work had been in the work force before, and that most wage-earning women needed and expected to continue working. The Moses report further heightened anxiety about women workers by implying that failure of women to "retire gracefully" would aggravate the postwar economic slump.

Paradoxically, at the same time that women were being encouraged to leave the work force at the end of the war, they were being courted by local industry with the promise of postwar jobs. Labor demands in the Portland-Vancouver region remained high during the second half of 1943 and the beginning of 1944, and the shipyards were recruiting women workers intensively. In this context it is not surprising that Henry Kaiser told an interviewer in *The New York Times* that he planned to hire women in the postwar period—"the ones who consider welding a better postwar achievement than wielding a typewriter or a broom. . . . I'm one who believes that 50 percent of women now in war work will stay in industry after the war," Kaiser said, "Do you think women are not going to demand the right to stay in industry?"[39]

Outside the shipyard, postwar prospects were a persistent theme in the competition for female workers during the labor shortage of 1943–44. Want ads like the following, exhorting women to plan for the postwar period, appeared frequently in the local newspapers throughout the period:

> Women who are dependent on their own work to learn a good trade in Zone Dry Cleaning Department. Positions will be good during and after the war.

> Young women are you looking to the future? Do you want a job that will continue? Investigate the opportunities of Pacific Telephone.[40]

The atmosphere of uncertainty sometimes propelled women shipyard workers to make plans which would afford them a more secure future. Dorothy Anderson and Ruth Drurey, for example, went to school during the war to prepare themselves for particular jobs in office work.[44]

The public in the Portland and Vancouver communities did not share the certainty of the Moses Committee about the plans of women war workers. While the advocates of women workers were not as visible in the Portland-Vancouver scene as they were nationally, a range of opinion could be found in the area. Throughout the latter part of 1943, speculations about the postwar plans of women workers filled local newspapers. "The biggest single question mark in the postwar employment picture is women," commented a magazine article in November 1943. "Will they want to return to the kitchens? If they should wish to continue working, how many will be employed and where? Men workers . . . want the answer. Some 7 million service men returning to the pursuits of peacetime would like this point cleared up. And so would the women themselves.[42]

In fact, the concern that this and other articles expressed was prompted by the *answers* that were coming in about the postwar intentions of women workers. An informal ballot had been inserted into the newspaper of one of the smaller shipyards in 1942 asking women workers to declare their postwar plans. *The Oregonian*, in reporting the results, highlighted the responses of the welders, 60 percent of whom planned to continue in the same kind of work after the war. "Other women workers," the article continued, "ranging from electricians to tarp sewers were 50 percent for staying in their jobs after victory."[43] Only the plans of industrial workers were described in the article and no explanation for the difference between women welders and other industrial workers was suggested. Perhaps the relatively high proportion of women welders in the shipyards nurtured hopes of postwar industrial work.

The facile predictions of the Moses report were most seriously challenged by the survey conducted in the three Kaiser yards by the Portland Committee on Postwar Planning in cooperation with labor unions, the Maritime Commission, and the shipyard management. Dr. Chilton Bush, chair of the department of journalism at Stanford University, designed the survey, which took place during the week of January 18, 1944 and included twenty-four questions. It consisted of personal interviews with 81,881 of the 91,036 employees at the three Kaiser shipyards – 91.5 percent of the workers employed that week. Because the researchers were primarily interested in the plans of families, only one spouse was interviewed when both husband and wife worked in the yard. The proportions of male and female married workers interviewed were equal. Women workers comprised 26.6 percent of the respondents.[44]

The main question that the survey sought to answer was how many of the workers who had recently come to the Portland area intended to stay. Researchers also sought four subsidiary kinds of information: (1) the skills that would be available in the postwar labor pool; (2) attitudes toward the Moses Plan; (3) "the number of field workers – especially women – who intended to remain in an industrial occupation after the war"; (4) the conditions that workers found inconvenient in the community.[45]

The interest of the survey committee in the plans of women field workers is significant. While all other questions in the survey were asked of all the workers interviewed, the question "Do you intend to stay in an industrial occupation after the war?" was preceded by the instruction "Ask of ALL FIELD EMPLOYEES ONLY (INCLUDING

WOMEN)" thereby excluding the approximately 11,593 office workers (14.2 percent of the participants) who were interviewed.[46] This vividly demonstrates that the concern was not whether women war workers would continue in the work force but whether those who were doing "male" jobs would want to continue doing them. There was little worry about whether there would be enough available jobs in office work after the war. In fact, there were indications that there would be a shortage of diversified clerical workers in the postwar period.[47]

The shipyard survey moved the subject of women's postwar plans out of the realm of speculation. Of the 16,322 women production workers who responded to the question "Do you intend to continue in an industrial job after the war?" over 53 percent responded positively, 35 percent negatively, and 8 percent were uncertain.[48] If over half of the women working at the smaller yards also planned to continue in industrial work, well over ten thousand women in the Portland and Vancouver area would be looking for industrial work after the war.

While the survey did not specify the marital status of the women who wanted to continue in industrial work, the public reacted to the survey results as if all women workers were married. *The Columbian* remarked gloomily, "Husbands who have awaited the end of hostilities in the expectation that welding wives would return to baking buns instead of building barges will find scant solace in Dr. Bush's revelation.[49] The *Bo's'n's Whistle* responded with transparent dismay and discussed the survey in a manner that was to characterize its treatment of women's postwar aspirations throughout the remainder of the war. After reporting that over half the women in the survey wanted to continue in industrial work after the war, the article selected the following quote from a welder at Oregon Ship, Mrs. Fern Webster: "I intend to return to my home. I believe a women who has an able-bodied husband should not work after the war is over. There will be plenty of returning soldiers to fill all the jobs which will be available."[50]

The response of the *Bo's'n's Whistle* inaugurated an assault on the postwar ambitions of female industrial workers that took various forms during the following two years and intensified as reconversion got under way. One form, as illustrated above, drew upon the Depression-bred prejudice against married women wage earners and the wartime loyalty to returning veterans. Articles about women workers frequently described women who planned to return to domesticity, and carried titles such as "Housewife's Working Days Limited by War." Dotting all three *Bo's'n's Whistle*s were poems and jokes that evoked images of the bygone days of femininity and domestic bliss, such as the following.

> Remember the days when girls wore skirts,
> And hats with feminine trimming?
> We hope that soon those days'll be back,
> And bring back our feminine women.[51]

Ten months after the major survey, the women's counseling department at Oregon Ship conducted another survey – this time focusing exclusively on women workers and their postwar plans. The sample was much smaller (872 women, most of whom were welders and electricians), and only one yard participated. Forty-five percent of the women in the survey (385) planned to continue in the same or a related line of work, a decline from the 53 percent of the earlier survey at Oregon Ship.[52] Since the size of the sample in the second survey was so much smaller than the first, firm conclusions cannot be drawn about changes in attitudes. The second poll does suggest, however, that the barrage of propaganda of the previous ten months may have had some effect on women workers. At any rate, the fact that another survey was conducted despite the comprehensiveness of the first suggests that the counseling department believed that the percentage of women who wanted to do industrial work after the war might have changed.

Most narrators had only vague recollections of their wartime expectations about the postwar period. It is difficult to reconstruct attitudes held in the past, particularly if those attitudes changed, became unpopular, or included unfulfilled expectations. Narrators' memories of the war were dominated by a sense of emergency. "I think," remembered Nell Conley, "as I believe most women did, that everything was in a state of suspension – 'after the war we'll see about this' – now we had to get busy and do what we had to do."[53] Loena Ellis agreed, describing the war as a "time out of living."[54] Etta Harvey, while she thought she might have continued the work had it been available, had no expectation that shipyard work would be a "permanent thing" for women. "My feeling was it was a job to get done to get our boys home and we had done our duty."[55] Twelve of the narrators indicated that they would have liked to continue in some form of industrial work after the war, but the negative messages were so loud and clear that none of them had expectations of being able to do so. Nona Pool recalled being informed by the union that women were being admitted because they needed the money, "but when the war was over you was out."[56] Jean Clark, when asked if she ever thought about continuing to do welding after the war, responded "Oh no, because women didn't do things like that. . . . I often thought about how wonderful it would be because they made such good money but there was no such thing as a woman ever being a welder. After that I don't think you could have gone out and gotten a job as a welder no matter how good you were."[57]

Despite this discouragement, however, there are some indications that women were taking training courses that would equip them for peacetime work in industry. Since there was little hope by late 1943 that shipbuilding would employ a significant number of workers in the Portland-Vancouver area after the war, those who wanted to continue in postwar industrial work needed skills that were applicable to peacetime industries such as housing construction and light metals. Most of the shipyard workers were trained in very specific skills applicable only to shipbuilding. Even ship repair work required more diversified training. Throughout 1944 and the first half of 1945, *Bo's'n's Whistles* for all three shipyards ran articles about the postwar prospects of the different crafts involved in shipbuilding, describing industries that were likely to employ workers in each craft and explaining the training needed.

Welding, the craft in which the largest number of women achieved journeymen status, was a relatively new skill, and a variety of peacetime industries were expected to use it with increased frequency. According to the *Bo's'n's Whistle*, over fifty jobs in peacetime industry could use welding skills, but welders would have a better chance of peacetime employment if they had more training than was normally provided for shipyard workers. By July 1944, increased training was available at two of the three yards, and Benson Polytechnical School offered a variety of welding courses. "These schools are for men and women alike," announced the Swan Island *Bo's'n's Whistle* in July 1944, "and according to Sylvester O'Grady, administrator in charge of Production Training, almost 80 percent of present trainees are women."[58] In the spring of 1945 the Boilermakers Union also began offering classes in response to popular demand.[59]

Many of the crafts that were used in shipbuilding were characterized by a rigid hierarchy delineated by tests, apprenticeships, and training programs. The electrical workers union, for example, issued journeyman "blue" cards to only 5 percent of the workers employed in the wartime shipbuilding industry. While the demand predicted for the postwar period was for journeyman electricians, most of the shipyard workers were working with "limited" cards which allowed them to do only certain kinds of work. Over a third of the electrical workers in the shipyards were women. The *Bo's'n's Whistle*, while observing that women have wondered where they would fit in after the war, noted that "opinion is almost unanimous that there is little hope for them as regular electricians. In 1930 there were only 38 women electricians in the entire United States. It isn't that they are barred because they are women, it is just that the field is normally unattractive, the work too heavy and the apprenticeship too tedious."[60] Women electricians' only hope, according to the *Bo's'n's Whistle*, was in work requiring a "class B" card. This was not really electrician work but involved assembling and repairing electrical parts. The prewar wage for such work was forty cents an hour. On close scrutiny, the article, typical of the way women's postwar aspirations were treated, makes very little sense. If women were one-third of the electricians in the wartime work force, then it seems inappropriate to base predictions about their postwar behavior on prewar statistics. If they were in fact wondering about their postwar prospects in the electrical field, one could easily deduce that many of them might be willing to take the additional training required to become journeymen. Two messages were communicated by such articles: (1) that women should not expect a place in peacetime industry; and (2) that women's postwar plans should not be based on wartime experiences.

The generally gloomy predictions about the postwar economy and the hierarchical nature of most shipyard crafts combined to create a climate that was inhospitable to the postwar aspirations of women industrial workers. Nevertheless, there is ample evidence that in 1943 a majority of women shipyard workers wanted to continue industrial work after the war. This evidence was not ignored. It stimulated a backlash on the part of policy-makers, male workers, and the press – a backlash that made it increasingly difficult for women to retain what were seen as deviant ambitions. Negative messages about women in industrial work proliferated, building toward a crescendo during the reconversion period. The intense hostility of the postwar environment to any nondomestic female ambition was, in part, a response to the information that many women had needs and aspirations that lay outside the home.

5 ☆ AFTER THE WAR

In a 1973 article entitled "What Really Happened to Rosie the Riveter?" Sheila Tobias and Lisa Anderson challenged the assumption that women war workers "retired gracefully" from their industrial jobs after the war. They documented the layoffs, the loopholes that were found to circumvent women's seniority rights, and the discrimination against women in peacetime industry concluding that "the quiescence of women in the fifties may well be the result not of Rosie's choice but of Rosie's frustration, which is another good reason for laying the myths surrounding Rosie the Riveter to rest."[1] Since the publication of this article, there has been disagreement among historians about women's responses to the reconversion process. Some researchers have argued that the patterns of the postwar world should be "seen as a choice by women" and point out that few women workers made a "public show of their displeasure" during the reconversion period.[2] Others have discovered women who protested the violation of women's seniority rights after the war and have argued that systematic harassment and intimidation prevented women from organizing against the sex discrimination of the reconversion period.[3]

Most of the research that explores women's responses to demobilization focuses on the industries organized by the United Auto Workers (UAW). While the UAW colluded with management after the war in the violation of women's seniority rights, it had promised protection of women workers during the war, and established a Women's Bureau within the union to address the problems of women workers. Women workers, therefore, had some expectation that their rights would be defended by their union after the war, and they had organizational support in the UAW Women's Bureau. It is not surprising that the incidents of explicit protest (a picket line, several grievances filed) should occur in an industry that gave lip service to the rights of women workers and promised its workers democratic decision-making and defense of their rights.[4]

In the Portland-Vancouver area, however, the metal trades unions, which consolidated their power in the shipyards early in the war, did not disguise their distrust of either women or blacks and did nothing to encourage the expectation that they would defend the postwar rights of women workers. As the previous chapter demonstrated, over half of the female industrial workers in the area's three largest shipyards reported in 1943 that they wanted to continue skilled industrial work after the war despite this hostile environment.

The four months after the war ended reveal a great deal about the situation confronting women wage earners, their attitudes toward reconversion, and the manner in which they made choices during the postwar period. During these four months thousands of women were forced out of skilled industrial work. Many of these women persistently refused to take the "women's" jobs offered to them at low wages until it became clear that they had no other choice. At that point they either took the lower-paying jobs, or, if they could afford it, dropped out of the work force. This pattern can be seen both nationally and in the Portland-Vancouver area.

The National Scene

It has been obvious," observed *Business Week* in November 1945," that the prewar law of supply and demand is operating badly in the labor market. Hosts of unemployed job seekers are simply refusing to take thousands of unfilled jobs in industry and that condition is exacting a toll on the nation's output of goods and services." One of the main features of the problem *Business Week* described was that "while most job openings are for men, most job seekers are women."[5] Since V-J Day the number of women employed as production workers in durable goods industries had declined precipitously, but the large number of women seeking work indicated that the wartime female labor force was not retiring en masse to resume its "domestic duties."[6]

Surveys demonstrated that most of the women working during the war (four out of five) needed to continue working "because of higher living costs or changed conditions at home" and that most female job seekers were looking for work in the fields in which they had been trained during the war.[7] They were not, however, finding such work, since the old barriers had been re-erected and women were universally excluded from the skilled industrial trades.[8] Most jobs available to women (40 to 61 percent in the three cities studied by the United States Employment Service (USES)) were in clerical and sales work and offered wages 43 to 52 percent lower than those last earned by the women applying for unemployment compensation. Many of the jobs offered to women in the postwar period were in industries and occupations that were not covered by the Fair Labor Standards Act and paid very low wages.[9] Throughout the first year after the war ended, employment and unemployment statistics indicated that women continued to avoid this kind of work. As a result there was a severe shortage of labor in fields that depended on a supply of cheap labor – the traditional employers of women. *Business Week* reported a "continuing personnel pinch on stores and restaurants, which lost, at peak, half of their women employees, and hotels and laundries, which saw two-thirds of their women workers leave for government shipyards and other duration jobs. The shortage of household help is also acute."[10] The demand for clerical workers had continued to expand and outstripped the supply of workers who had clerical experience.[11]

By June 1946, national labor market statistics suggest that most women workers had abandoned hope. The number of people being added to payrolls was finally equal to those being laid off. The new jobs taken by women, however, were in those fields that women workers had been attempting to avoid for the previous six months.[12] Women over thirty-five, who had joined the workforce in large numbers during the war, faced increasing discrimination and remained unemployed longer.[13]

The number of women unable to find the jobs they wanted and the discrimination against older women workers support Paddy Quick's suggestion that the decline in the number of women in the work force from 19.3 million in 1945 to 15.8 million in 1947 can be at least partially attributed to the number of female job seekers who became discouraged and dropped out of the work force.[14] The unwillingness of women to take traditionally female low-paid jobs in the years after the end of the war suggests that for a while women workers resisted the process by which they were being forced to re-enter the female ghetto in the job market. A detailed examination of the Portland-Vancouver area will illuminate this pattern.

"Everyone Was Out of Sync"

During the first half of 1945 the atmosphere in the Portland and Vancouver shipyards was tense and anxious. Although the shipyard management assured workers that enough ships had been contracted to maintain employment through 1945, employment at all the shipyards declined steadily, provoking occasional outbursts of anger at the union hiring hall.[15] The shipyard management denied rumors that more women were being laid off than men, claiming that they were only terminating workers with high absentee rates, but the Postwar Readjustment and Development Commission of Oregon reported that in early 1945 the shipyards had "discharged hundreds of absentees, women, and workers over 60 years."[16] In May 82 percent of the workers applying for unemployment compensation in the Portland area were women, which the Readjustment Commission saw as indicative of the drive away from the shipyards, for most of the claims filed in Portland were by ex-shipyard workers."[17] The termination of several women counselors at the Swan Island yard in February signaled the beginning of the end of the era in which women were seen as an essential part of the shipyard workforce.[18]

In April, Oregon Ship received a contract for the construction of aluminum pontoons and assigned about 3,200 workers to work on them. Pontoon work consisted mainly of riveting, and 80 percent of the workers assigned to it were women. The pontoon work was the last shipyard work for many of the women at Oregon Ship. According to a USES report of June 1945, the shipyard management planned to offer the women working on the pontoons an opportunity to work on new ship construction in the boilermaker trades mostly as welder trainees or boilermakers' helpers. Since this would involve working for wages that were considerably lower than what they had been making for pontoon work, the report predicted that "a good proportion of these women will withdraw from the labor market rather than accept work at a lower pay scale. Outside the shipbuilding industry there will be plenty of work in the area for women when this aluminum pontoon contract is completed. Particularly this is true of the food processing and canning industry."[19] The report did not point out, however, that the wages of food processing and canning work were usually far below that of trainees and helpers in the boilermaker trades.

The mounting anxiety about layoffs intensified male hostility toward female shipyard workers. Nona Pool, for example, an Oregon Ship welder, had been riveting on the pontoons and was transferred back to the ways without any explanation in May 1945. "The yard," she remembered, "was in a turmoil."

> Everyone was cranky there too. I hadn't welded for so long I was rusty – got "flack" from "all men crew" – and told to go wash "didies" etc. I finally got to the ship supervisor and told him and he helped me get transferred back to the pontoons, as he said he saw no reason why I was singled out for the ways – "just some bigshot shuffling." I guess everyone was "out of sync" knowing the yard was in the process of shutting down.[20]

By May 1945, the *Bo's'n's Whistle* had abandoned any pretense of neutrality when discussing women's postwar future. In blithe contradiction to the information supplied by the comprehensive survey the magazine had reported six months earlier, it headlined a May article, " 'The Kitchen' – Women's Big Post-War Goal." The article began with the following description of the author's conception of women's views:

> Brothers, the tin hat and welder's torch will be yours! We, the women, will give them back to you with best regards. In the post-war future we will probably be able to give you many little tips on their proper care and use, but when the war finally is won the thing we want to do is take off these unfeminine garments and button ourselves into something starched and pretty.[21]

The article, based on interviews with 100 women at Oregon Ship, reported that questioners were constantly interrupted by male workers insisting, "They ought to go home. Women haven't any business trying to do man's work."[22] The message for women workers was that any ambition to continue in industrial work was deviant and threatening to men.

As the war drew to a close, contracts for new ships expired and several of the shipyards shifted to ship repair work. Ship repair work, unlike shipbuilding, had not been broken down into specific tasks and still required diversified training. According to a representative of Commercial Iron Works, there was "considerable dissatisfaction" among the one thousand women production workers at Commercial because only men were being transferred to repair work, which paid higher wages and was expected to last another two years. Repair work, according to the Commercial representative was "not suitable for women."[23]

After V-J Day any remaining uncertainty about the position of women in the postwar industrial world had vanished. The metal trades unions made it clear to management, the War Labor Board, and the USES that they supported the retention of men only for the shrinking pool of jobs. All of the shipyards in the area pursued a policy of laying women off before men. In August a representative of Willamette Iron and Steel (WISCO) reported to the Multnomah County Day Care Committee that "forced reductions at WISCO have been mostly women. The prediction at Willamette is that in sixty days practically no women will be left in the yards."[24] Between July 15 and September 1, 1945, the number of workers employed by the shipbuilding industry in the area declined by 30 percent, while the number of women employed in area shipbuilding declined by 41 percent. The USES predicted even sharper declines in female employment in October and November.[25]

For many women shipyard workers the end of the war brought a sense of being jolted back to reality. The war was, in the recollections of several of the narrators, a time in which normal rules didn't apply. "The shipyards was a little different," recalled Virginia Larson as she was describing the changed mood after the war. "It was really quite different from real life. You didn't get treated the same as you did otherwise – in normal life."[26] Some assumed that as soon as the war ended prewar rules would be re-established. "I guess I just figured," Mabel Studebaker commented, "that it was just part of the times. . . . They didn't hire 'em before the war and I figured they didn't hire 'em after the war either."[27] By the end of the war, popular sentiment against women working in traditionally male jobs had reached such intensity that most women saw the handwriting on the wall. The day after the war ended Edna Hopkins was working in the pipe shop, and everyone stopped to gather around the radio to hear the victory news. Hopkins went back to finish her pipe.

> So the boss he comes over and says, "Shorty, what are you doing working on that pipe?" He says, "You can do that tomorrow, . . . the war is over. There's no hurry now. Nobody's working but you." And I said, "Well, I want to finish this pipe." I said, "This is the last pipe I'll ever weld." And he laughed and he said, "You're kidding, Shorty, you'll be here tomorrow." I said, "You wanna bet?" and he said "Yeah, I'll bet." "Okay, name your bet." And he walked away and I went ahead and finished my pipe and that was the last pipe I ever welded. They laid me off the next day. . . . The women in the pipe shop were all laid off.[28]

But while women workers may not have been surprised that they were the first to be laid off, the sudden shift in the atmosphere did not go unnoticed. "It seemed like after the war," recalled Virginia Larson, "there was just nothing for women because they just – I don't know – there just weren't enough jobs perhaps – I don't know. I just don't think they thought that much of women. . . . Suddenly if you were to say you were a machinist – you'd be laughed at . . . or they'd say, Well, there's too many men that need work, or Why don't you stay home or do something else?"[29] And despite all the preparation and resignation, losing a job was frightening. "You kind of get a sunken feeling in the pit of your stomach 'cause that was your job," commented Larson.[30]

Most of the metal trades unions terminated women's membership after the war on the grounds that they had been temporary workers. "They'd let us in," commented Nona Pool. "They let us pay dues, but if we'd have tried to get a job in the Boilermakers we'd have gotten laughed off the face of the earth." Pool's withdrawal card read, "for the purposes of housewife."[31]

Women shipyard workers reacted in a variety of ways to the abrupt termination of their war jobs. While many of them indicated that they would have stayed in industrial work after the war, Nell Conley was one of the few who remember feeling what she described as "straight blazing anger" when her union membership was terminated. "When your union cards were pulled there was no way that a woman could get into any of those heavy industries. I knew women who were working as electricians, as shipfitters, a number of other jobs out there. Of course all of them were pulled, not just the welders."[32]

LueRayne Culbertson had never really expected to continue welding, but she remembers with pleasure that, although the union "wanted your union card immediately, I never did turn in my union card. I still got it."[33] "When the war was over," recalls Reva Baker, "the Boilermakers did not want the women in the union. They did not want them working in men's jobs. They didn't feel that women were qualified for men's jobs even though we had been doing it all during the war. They were trying to protect the men and their jobs."[34]

Loena Ellis would have liked to have been a machinist after the war, but "they were not allowing women to retain their status in the machinists union." She did, however, confront the business agent of her union, who refused to issue her a withdrawal card on the assumption that she would never want to rejoin the union so she might as well leave without an official withdrawal. Knowing that this would mean a hefty fee if she ever did want to rejoin, Ellis insisted on her withdrawal card.[35]

Betty Cleator had the opposite reaction. She worked as a draftsman at the shipyards and would have liked to have continued after the war. It was clear to her, however, that there was no chance of her continuing in drafting, so when she was charged for a withdrawal she responded, "You can give me an honorable withdrawal through my last payment, or you can forget it, because I've paid all the money to this union I'm going to. You can't get me a job; you can't even get me references to one."[36]

"Adjusting" to Reconversion

"When the shipyard was over," commented Jean Clark, "that was it. There was no other place. You went back as either a waitress or worked in an office or something like that. . . . Nobody would have hired a women to weld anything after the shipyards. I don't care how many years of experience you'd had. Nobody would have hired you. That was a man's job."[37]

As peacetime industries begin hiring, the sex-segregated labor market reassumed its prewar contours. Most plants that had hired women in historically male jobs during the war were replacing them with male workers. Women were almost completely excluded from the newly available skilled jobs even in industries in which shortages of male workers were reported, such as railroad, logging, and aluminum fabrication.

The women shipyard workers who looked for jobs during this period found themselves confronted with the following choices: (1) they could stay in the labor force and work in canneries, poultry and egg processing, textiles, sales, or services; (2) they could retrain themselves to qualify for the available clerical jobs, which were requiring more training than they had before the war; or (3) they could drop out of the work force.

The wages for most jobs available to women contrasted sharply with the wages of shipyard production jobs, the lowest of which paid 80 cents per hour. "You were back to women's wages, you know," commented Marie Schreiber, "practically in half."[38] Cannery work was seasonal, and in 1945 was paying 66 cents per hour for women and 80 to 85 cents per hour for men; domestic work paid a maximum of $75 a month plus room and board. Clerical salaries ranged from 75 cents to $1.40 an hour depending on skill and experience. Among the highest salaries available to women were those paid to power machine operators in garment factories. These jobs were piecework, and it was possible to earn $10 to $12 a day, but many women avoided them because of the intense pressure and monotony of the work.[39]

Oral history recollections of women who looked for employment after the war vividly illustrate the situation confronting women workers. Nell Conley's husband didn't return from the service for seven months after the war ended, and she had a young child to support. During the war she had believed that it was most important to get the ships built and inappropriate to worry about postwar problems. But as she began to look for other work she became angry at the union's exclusion of women shipyard workers. "There were very few places," she recalled, "very few jobs women could take where their salary was anywhere near what a man's would have been for the same kind of work, and there were many, many kinds of work that were simply out of bounds for women."[40] According to Mabel Studebaker, "There wasn't any jobs for women except when the canneries would start up; then I worked at the canneries. . . . I did not like cannery work."[41] The food processing industry, an important element in the economy of the Northwest was (and is) an employer of thousands of women at low wages. During the war the local canneries had been so desperate for labor, that they had enlisted the help of the USES and War Manpower Commission in a door-to-door recruitment drive. Hoping to attract women workers, two new canneries located in the Portland area shortly after the end of the war, one of them at the site of a large housing development that had been built for shipyard workers. The employment figures for women in the two years following the war fluctuated with the canning season, reaching a peak from August to November and then declining.[42] Edna Hopkins, who shared Studebaker's distaste for the canneries, was collecting unemployment compensation when the cannery season began. "I did collect unemployment insurance," she remembers, "and they made me go to work in the cannery and whatever before I ever got very much of it."[43]

In January 1946, the USES reported a problem matching applicants with available jobs. Three-quarters of the jobs available paid wages below the prevailing rates in the community, and some of them were even considered substandard. The remaining jobs were for machinists, mechanics, stenographers, engineers, and electricians, but they could not be filled because employers had become very specific about qualifications.[44] Qualifications for industrial jobs usually involved the diversified training of an all-round journeyman; for the stenographer jobs, the requirements included skill, experience and age.[45]

Mr. Kerrick, the Portland supervisor of USES, contended that "a very lenient attitude has been assumed in determining whether or not a job opening was "suitable" employment and whether or not the claimant could rightfully be considered 'available' for work." On the other hand, Kerrick made it clear that war-acquired skills were not taken seriously into consideration in determining the "suitability" of jobs for men or women.

Both men and women were included among the job seekers who were either unacceptable to employers or unwilling to settle for lower-paying jobs, and men also found themselves unable to adapt their shipyard skills to the peacetime labor market.[47] Women, however, presented particular problems when, according to the placement director of the USES, their expectations had been raised unrealistically by the war. One group the USES placed in this category was composed of young women who had entered the work force during the war after quitting or graduating from high school and had insufficient training for the jobs available for women after the war. In the other problem group were women who left other jobs to work in the defense industry and were reluctant to return to their former occupations. According to the USES placement director, "These women present a major problem and the USES has not been able to do too much in adjusting these women to the reconversion period."[48]

Among the women who had most difficulty "adjusting to reconversion" were black women and women in the "higher age brackets" (over thirty-five). In her study of women wage earners in four cities, Lois Helmbold demonstrated that during the Depression women who were black and/or over thirty-five were displaced by younger, white workers.[49] During the war older women moved back into the work force, and black women of all ages moved from domestic and service work to industrial work. In the reconversion period, these women, whom Helmbold described as being "on the bottom of the employment hierarchy," confronted the restoration of prewar conditions.[50]

About half of the black population left the Portland-Vancouver area after the war, and those that remained faced widespread discrimination by employers and unions. The USES did not force employers to hire black workers, because employers threatened to find workers elsewhere. USES officials concluded that it was "unwise and the wrong approach to attempt to force employers to hire colored workers against their will" after thirty firms stopped using USES during the war when they were pressured to hire black workers. Members of the Portland chapter of the Urban League, which had been established during the war, thought that USES workers themselves lacked "racial tolerance" and were not doing enough to change the policies of local industries. Portland, according to Urban League members, was the most bigoted city on the West Coast.[51]

Black women, of course, faced double discrimination. Only two Portland area manufacturing establishments registered with the USES would employ black women: a garment factory and a bag factory that operated two segregated buildings, one for white workers and the other for black workers. The Urban League tried to improve employment prospects for black workers by pressuring unions and employers to end discriminatory practices and by reluctantly acting as an employment agency for black workers. (Urban League staff members felt that the USES dumped unemployed black workers on them.) Black women seeking the help of the USES or the Urban League were often urged to take work in domestic service, which "most of them are reluctant to do . . . because they object to the wage scales and the working conditions." According to the USES, many of the black women looking for work were married and unable to live at their place of employment, a requirement for many domestic jobs.

Margaret Kay Anderson, field secretary for the Women's Bureau reported that "many of the colored women who worked during the war are out of the labor market because they had no intention of working when the war was over."[52] She did not explain how the USES knew that these women had been planning to retire from the work force and were not discouraged by the limited opportunities for black women workers. Since wages were low and unemployment high for black male workers, it seems reasonable to assume that many black women would be looking for work.

Nationally, women over thirty-five, to whom Margaret Kay Anderson referred as "women whose services in the labor market are no longer needed," composed 45 percent of the female labor force in 1944.[53] Almost three-quarters of the women filing unemployment claims at the beginning of 1948 in the state of Oregon were over thirty, and 44 percent of the female claimants were over forty.[54] At the same time, there was an accumulation of "hard-to-fill" jobs in stenographic, office, and clerical work because women were unable to "meet the rigid employer specifications as to skill, experience and age, particularly the latter requirement."[55] "A high percentage of job openings," reported the Portland-Vancouver Unemployment Bulletin for December 1948, "now specify that applicants should not be over thirty-five or forty years of age."[56]

For the next three years after the end of the war, the USES reported that many workers were still looking for jobs in the trades in which they had been trained during the war but were not acceptable to employers because they did not satisfy the requirements for "all-around journeyman." Simultaneously, many jobs characterized by low wage scales and long hours, such as janitorial work, domestic work, and sales, were unfilled.

Meanwhile, inflation was straining the resources of wage-earning and job-seeking women. Between 1946 and 1947, the cost of living increased 15 percent, while the salaries for most jobs available for women paid under a dollar an hour.[58] Marie Schreiber commented that it took two people's wages "to make headway. I mean one person, you just couldn't make it."[59]

The interviews with women shipyard workers tell the human stories behind the "unbalanced" labor market statistics of the late 1940s. Of the thirty-five narrators, five left the work force after the war to raise children and re-entered later in their lives; two worked with their husbands on a farm and in a shop. As the Women's Bureau often pointed out, the majority of women who had been working during the war needed to continue working, and this was true for the women we interviewed as well. The nature of their needs varied from case to case, but they all described themselves as needing to earn money. Most women eventually found jobs in clerical, sales, service, and textile work but as the USES records indicate, they did not adjust easily to the limited opportunities they faced.

Several of the women worried about finding work that was more permanent than shipyard work and took steps as the end of the war approached to either make themselves more marketable or find more stable positions. Kathryn Blair, who was supporting herself, her child, and her mother-in-law, left the shipyards before the war ended. "I needed to get into something where I would have some stability–a steady job." She moved back to her family farm and got a job doing office work in Vancouver.[60] Ruth Drurey and Dorothy Anderson, who had gone to school during the war to learn bookkeeping and stenography, were able to get jobs using these skills after the war and worked their way up to management in the 1950s and 1960s.

Katherine Baker quit her welding job at Commercial Iron Works before the war ended. She explained,

> I did enjoy working there and everything, but I thought it looked like it was winding down, and when it starts winding down, you got 30,000 people in Oregon and 15,000 there, another 30,000 over here in Willamette, and–well that's over 100,000 people in all these plants –and when they shut down, then what? There wouldn't be enough work for half of the men, and the men would be hired first. Then when the boys come back from the war, they'd just automatically make a place for them. You'd better find a niche, says I to me. I thought there wouldn't be any of these soldier boys lining up to be grocery clerks, and that's what I decided to be.[62]

Baker was not the only one leaving the shipyards to look for permanent work. The yards were not letting workers leave easily. Baker managed to get a clearance after "getting obnoxious" and found a job at a grocery store near her house.[63]

Office work was one of the few expanding fields for women. During the 1940s and 1950s it still offered some opportunities for advancement and attracted women who were looking for a career after the war. Betty Cleator, for example, had obtained a degree in landscape architecture before the war, but found that the field was closed to women on all levels. There were few jobs doing actual landscape architecture and there was "a lot of discrimination" against women. Most landscape architects, according to Cleator, entered the field by working in greenhouses–work inaccessible to women. "The only thing women did in greenhouses," commented Cleator, "was to decorate the poinsettias for Christmas." When she found herself unable to find a job, Cleator's father paid for her to attend a business college for two months, and, in her words, "I made my living punching a typewriter ever since." The war period, when she worked as a draftsman, was the only time in her life that she used any of the training from her college career.[64]

Loena Ellis remembers the period after the war as one of unrest for many people who couldn't decide "what direction to take. And in a way I was in that boat too, because I definitely wasn't going to go back to the factory, and the machinist work was gone, so it was sort of starting over fresh for me." She did try for a short time to find a job in which she could use some of her training as a machinist, but the only job she could find was in camera repair, which seemed too confining to her. She therefore decided "it couldn't hurt to learn about the business world" and attended business college for a year to study bookkeeping.[65] Virginia Larson, also realizing there was no opportunity for women machinists, used her shipyard savings to go to business college and learn bookkeeping.[66] Both Larson and Ellis saw office training as a means of escaping factory work.

For Marie Schreiber, adjusting to reconversion meant accepting the low wages that, according to USES officials, deterred many women from taking jobs in sales and service. Schreiber and her sister, Betty Niederhaus, both eventually found retail jobs, one cashiering at a variety store and the other in sales at Sears. "After the shipyards were over," Schreiber commented, "then you have to take a big cut in pay. It kind of hurt."[67]

The largest unfilled need in the Portland-Vancouver area for women workers throughout 1946 was for power machine operators in the textile industries. The postwar consumption boom had boosted business in the region's garment industry, creating a critical labor shortage. There were six large textile mills and about fifteen small manufacturing companies in Portland and Vancouver. Most of these operated on a piecework system. Although experienced operators could earn wages that compared favorably to those typical of women's work, textile work did not attract workers.[68] Several of the narrators ended up working in the textile industry in the 1950s, but only two took these jobs immediately after the war. Their comments shed light on the reasons women avoided textile work. "I hated it," commented Pat Rowlands about her job at Jantzen Knitting Mills. "I despised it. But I was a good operator, and the gals said, 'As long as you're making a lot of money, what do you care?' I said, 'Hey, I gotta get more out of my job than this.'" Rowlands' shipyard experience, which she referred to as "the only experience that I had that I really liked," had given her a taste of a job she enjoyed.[69] All of the narrators who worked in textile mills at any point in their lives commented on the speed, the tedium, and the pressure of mill work.[70]

Despite efforts to find alternatives, two of the three black women worked as domestics in the postwar period. Audrey Moore, who was the sole support of her child, reported having difficulty finding jobs – a difficulty compounded by being female and black, and by not having a high-school education. Housecleaning, poultry work, and seasonal cannery work were all she could find.[71] Marie Merchant cleaned Pullman cars for a while and then did domestic work for private families.[72] Beatrice Marshall, the narrator who had been trained as a machinist but was a victim of racial discrimination in the shipyards, worked at the bag factory until it closed in 1946, when she got a job as a page in the public library.[73]

Both the statistical evidence and the oral history material demonstrate that the reconversion period was one of enormous difficulty for women who worked in industrial jobs during the war and remained in the work force. Suddenly the temporary respect women experienced in the shipyards vanished, and the options available to them contracted dramatically. For many women the return to "normalcy" made what one historian has described as "the deferred middle-class dream of family, security, and upward mobility" less accessible.[74]

Labor market statistics demonstrate that in the immediate postwar period in the Portland-Vancouver area, women who were shut out of skilled industrial work avoided the low-paid, tedious, and high-pressure work that depended on female labor for as long as they could. While protests against the unfair treatment of women workers may not have taken the form of litigation, direct action, or organization, it was manifested in women's stubborn refusal to "adjust to reconversion."

Reconversion and Child Care

The position of women in the postwar work force was intimately connected with the future of programs to care for the children of working mothers. In the wartime atmosphere of change and possibility – an environment that engendered both fears and fantasies – there was some discussion about continuing one of the Kaiser centers during the postwar period. Like other optimistic ideas about the position of women in the work force, this one evaporated in the postwar climate of conservatism. Even during the war, the advocates of permanent care for the children of working mothers were a minority in the Portland area. The dominant view among professional educators was exemplified by *Survey Mid Monthly*, which, in an article acclaiming the Kaiser Child Service Centers, hastened to add, "But after the war, the whole subject of the care of children of working mothers will have to be reconsidered. More weight can be given then to the argument that the young child's place is in his home with his mother."[75]

The functionalist assumption that domestic mothers were essential to the smooth working of family and society shaped post war approaches to child care. To the extent that the wartime experience with working mothers affected the attitudes of education and social work professionals, it was within this functionalist framework. For example, David Levy, in "The War and Family Life," noted that some mothers had better relationships with their children when they played "less than the usual maternal role" and were engaged in activities outside the home. Jobs outside the home, according to Levy, provided an opportunity for these women to resolve this difficulty, but he insisted that "as adjustments of difficulties, they are for the most part temporary devices." Levy's assertion that "the most frequent source of family disintegration . . . is the absent or neglectful mother" typifies the consensus that emerged in the professional literature in the postwar period.

> Mothers of infants up to age three should be barred from factory work. Mothers of the preschool child should be allowed employment only during the periods in which a nursery school, properly inspected, took over. In any case, until the child is fourteen years old, a job longer than six hours is a questionable undertaking for a mother who has full care of her children.[77]

Reflecting these attitudes, the Federal Works Agency, which was administering federal funding for child-care centers, announced in August 1945 that since women workers were no longer needed for the war effort, all funding for child-care centers would be terminated by October 1945.[78] Simultaneously, the money stopped flowing into the Kaiser Child Service Centers. Since the centers had been funded by the Maritime Commission as part of the costs of ship construction, they were slated to close in September 1945 as the last ship construction contracts were being fulfilled.[79]

While the members of the day-care committees in the Portland-Vancouver area were influenced by the prevailing ideology about young children, many of them were directors of child-care agencies and were in daily contact with the realities of women's lives. As the end of the war approached, they became increasingly concerned about the women who would have to continue working and might find themselves stranded when the federal funding for child care was cut off. Despite the massive layoffs of women shipyard workers, thousands of women remained in the work force and needed child care. Early in its existence, the Oregon Child-Care Committee had agreed that it would not terminate at the end of the war but would continue to monitor the care and protection of children in the postwar period.[80] In June 1945, the Multnomah County Day Care Committee established a subcommittee for postwar planning.[81]

During the summer of 1945, there were 2,500 children enrolled in child-care centers in Portland and Vanport; 1,850 were enrolled in centers funded by the Lanham Act, 455 were in the Kaiser centers, and 195 were in privately funded agencies. Since the private centers were almost full to capacity and the Kaiser centers were due to close in September, over 2,000 children would be left without care when the Lanham Act funds were withdrawn.[82]

Communities throughout the country were facing a similar crisis, and emergency committees sprang up to pressure Congress to extend the Lanham Act support for child-care centers.[83] The Women's Auxiliaries of the CIO were spearheading the campaign, and Nathalie Panek, a local representative of the CIO war relief committee, encouraged the Vancouver and Oregon child-care groups to participate.[84] The Multnomah County Day Care Committee formed a special committee to mobilize support, issued statements, wired congressmen, sent a representative (Saidie Dunbar) to Washington to lobby, and worked closely with Oregon Senator Wayne Morse, who campaigned for the extension of federal aid to child care throughout the summer and fall of 1945.[85]

Even while campaigning to save the child-care centers, the members of the day-care committee remained ambivalent about providing support for wage-earning mothers. Periodic disagreements arose within the committee about whether any mothers of young children should be working in the postwar period and whether child care would encourage mothers to work.[86] By emphasizing the needs of the wives of servicemen who had not yet returned from duty, the day-care committee could remain unified and present their campaign as a response to a war-created emergency.[87] Reports from the child-care centers during the last four months of 1945 made it clear, however, that only about a third of the women using the existing child-care centers were servicemen's wives or war widows.[88] Clearly, the child-care centers were meeting a need that went beyond the effects of the war. Clients of the child-care centers, regardless of their situation, were communicating in a variety of ways that they depended on the centers and were distressed by their imminent termination. One group of distressed mothers forced the Guild's Lake Center to reopen after it had closed.[89]

All committee members agreed that women who were the sole or main support of their families should not be forced to go on welfare because of the absence of child care. This addressed the situation of approximately 25 percent of the women who were using the centers in Multnomah County. The consensus that emerged, after considerable discussion, about the rest of the women who were using the centers was similar to the adaptation of functionalist analysis articulated by David Levy. Since committee members saw themselves as representing the interests of children, they presented the child-care centers as a solution to the problems posed by those women who "can accept motherhood but reject their children if they have to stay home and take care of them." They observed that their clients were distressed by the instability of the child-care programs and its effect on their work lives, and they feared that the mothers' distress would turn to resentment that "would be reflected in the children who need protection against undesirable attitudes."[90]

The efforts to extend Lanham Act funds were successful only in forestalling the cutoff day until March 1, 1946. President Truman, in recommending extension of funding for the Federal Works Project Child Care program, framed the measure clearly as a temporary expedient necessary to allow communities time to assume financial responsibility for their child-care programs.[91] Since few states or cities were prepared to make a substantial commitment to child care, this left most programs without support. Howard Dratch argues that the campaign to continue funding for postwar child care ultimately failed because it was abandoned by the national labor movement and the national child-welfare establishment.[92] The ambivalence of the campaign itself, as exemplified by the Multnomah County Day Care Committee, may well have been a contributing factor. While a group of CIO women were prepared to argue for peacetime child care, their's was a minority position within the campaign, which otherwise pushed only for temporary measures to deal with the effects of the war.[93]

The child-care committees in the Portland-Vancouver area attempted to obtain funding from private agencies, local boards of education, and the governments of Washington and Oregon. Private agencies contributed some funding, but little was forthcoming from the states. The Vanport and Vancouver boards of education took over a few of the centers, but most of the community centers were left without public funding when federal funds were terminated.[94] Just at the point when women workers were taking huge cuts in wages, child-care center fee scales were raised. Most of the highly-trained child-care professionals who were attracted by the high wages and exciting possibilities at the Kaiser centers left the area because of the low salaries offered at community child-care centers. At one privately operated nursery school the teachers were extremely distressed because they were making less than the janitorial staff, which was unionized, and several of them resigned in protest against the low wages and long hours.[95]

Throughout 1945 and 1946 the number of available child-care programs declined. State licensing procedures contributed to the difficulty of keeping child-care centers alive. During the war a liberal licensing code had been in effect, but with the end of the war the more stringent prewar codes were revived, and several of the public nursery schools that had been operating under the wartime codes could no longer satisfy the requirements. The prewar code in Oregon, for example, made it illegal for nursery schools to operate in basements, which eliminated several of the Portland centers that were using the basements of churches.[96]

Of the twenty public child-care centers available in Portland in 1945, only seven were still active in July 1946. Enrollment at the remaining centers increased throughout the fall of 1945 and the spring of 1946, although only two centers were full to capacity, one of which was the only center in the black community. The fact that all the centers were not full to capacity may have been a result of parents' uneasiness about the instabilitiy of the centers. Cuts in funding were imminent from September to March; after March conditions were even more unstable and a number of centers closed.

Shrinking child-care facilities in the Portland area strained the resources of working mothers and their families, forcing some of them to send their children to foster homes and others to abandon their jobs. The situation of the children in the Mt. Scott Day Care Center, one of centers closed after the Lanham Act funds were cut, illustrates the dilemma facing wage-earning mothers. Of the forty-nine children who had attended, thirteen were sent to foster homes, ten were cared for by relatives, and three went to work with their mothers. Nine children were transferred to other child-care centers but the center that received eight of these children closed four months later. Nine mothers quit their jobs, and two were on unemployment.[97]

While this situation narrowed the choices for all women, it was most destructive for those who were the sole support of their families.

According to surveys conducted in 1945 and 1946 between 22 and 25 percent of the mothers of children in the Portland centers were the sole or main support of their families.[98] Of the 105 mothers of children at the Volunteers of America center in April 1946 (one of the centers that closed the following summer), 55 were widowed, separated or divorced.[99]

When the Kaiser Child Service Centers closed, the *Bo's'n's Whistle* published a retrospective on the centers, voicing the hopes of their staff that "one result of the centers' good operation will be the spread of some of these ideas to other industries and other communities so that workers elsewhere and Kaiser workers returning to their home communities will find similar facilities being developed as a result of the experiment here."[100] But in the Portland-Vancouver area, child-care facilities contracted radically, and the memory of the wartime child care programs of which the day-care committees had been so proud soon faded.

"An Era Gone By"

When the Northwest Women's History Project began interviewing women who had worked in the shipyards, we were impressed by how eager women were to talk about their shipyard experience. Throughout the process of interviewing, producing a slide show, and gathering former shipyard workers for a reunion, the women commented on the lack of recognition they felt in the preceding thirty-five years. One narrator, Helen Berggren, commented, "I thought I'd die before someone remembered us."[101] Many narrators felt a sense of disjunction between their shipyard days, when they felt they were part of publicly recognized effort to win the war, and the rest of their lives—private and unglorious. Their interviews were sprinkled with comments such as LueRayne Culbertson's reflection that when she "walked out of the shipyard, that was it. Just like you pull a curtain down. . . . That's an era gone by."[102]

To avoid perpetuating this sense of discontinuity between the World War II era and the rest of women's lives, *Fleeting Opportunities* will conclude with a brief examination of the world of women wage earners in the Portland-Vancouver area in 1950 and some glimpses of the postwar lives of a few of the narrators. It will begin with an overview of the changes in the female labor force in the Portland-Vancouver area between 1940 and 1950 and will then examine, through the recollections of the former shipyard workers, two different strands of female experience in the postwar work world.

Wage-Earning Women in 1950

In some respects, the world that women in the Portland-Vancouver area inhabited in 1950 was very different from the prewar world. The community had become more urban and more densely populated. Despite the radical contraction of the shipbuilding industry, most of the workers who had come to the area for shipyard jobs remained, causing the population of the Portland metropolitan area to double and that of Vancouver to triple between 1940 and 1950.[103]

As in the rest of the country, many more women were in the work force. In both Portland and Vancouver, the percentage of women working for wages had lagged behind national figures before the war but increased more than 5 percent between 1940 and 1950 – slightly more than the rest of the country.[104] As in the country as a whole, the most dramatic change in the female work force over the decade was the increasing number of married women who were working for wages. In 1940, only 17.5 percent of all married women in Portland had been employed compared to 27.4 percent in 1950.[105] Some married women had left the work force after the war, but many returned soon after, and many others began working later in the decade. The permanent retirement of the "housewives turned welders" that some people had predicted did not materialize.

The occupational distribution of the female work force, however, had much more in common with prewar than with wartime patterns. Women had virtually disappeared from what was left of the shipbuilding industry. The Kaiser Corporation left the area in 1947, and the other shipyards reduced their work forces radically. By 1950 there were only 469 people employed in shipbuilding in Portland. Thirty-two of these workers were women, but only five of them were production workers. The census figures of 1950 testify to the failure of women's efforts to use their war-acquired skills in peacetime industry. Female craftsmen, foremen, and kindred workers represented only 1 percent of all working women in the area in both 1940 and 1950. The welders, burners, helpers, and sweepers of the wartime period had moved into the restaurants and typing pools of the 1950s.[106]

In Portland, which emerged from the war as a major commercial center, the largest segment of the female wage-earning population was employed in clerical and sales work; this segment increased from 39 percent in 1940 to 42 percent in 1950. Clerical and sales occupations provided an alternative to service work, the second most common female occupation. The average clerical salary paid a little over $1.00 an hour, while the average hourly wage for service workers was under 70 cents. As in the country as a whole, fewer women were doing domestic work, which employed only 6 percent of women wage earners in 1950 as compared to 11 percent in 1940. Nondomestic service work declined slightly, employing 16 percent of all women workers in 1940 and 15 percent in 1950.[107]

In Vancouver, which remained a small town with less commerce and industry than its neighbor, the service sector expanded more than office work. The number of Vancouver women working at clerical jobs actually declined from 31 to 28 percent while those employed in service work grew from 16 to 18 percent. The new garment factory that opened in Vancouver after the war increased the percentage of women working as operatives from 9 to 12 percent, while the percentage of domestic workers declined from 10 to 6 percent.[108]

The expanded opportunities in clerical and sales work were not accessible to most black women, who did not fare well in the postwar period in the Portland-Vancouver area. The proportion of black women who worked as domestics declined less than it did in most other northern cities; most employed black women continued to work at service jobs, and while more black women found jobs in factories, they were a small proportion of all black women wage earners. In Portland 18 percent of the non-white female labor force was unemployed as compared to 6 percent of white wage-earning women, while in Vancouver, twenty-eight of the ninety-one non-white women in the labor force (30 percent) were unemployed in 1950.[109]

Women over 35 comprised more than half of the female labor force, increasing in Portland from 49 to 59 percent, but they too were underrepresented in the expanding clerical sector. While 46 percent of the wage-earning women were working in clerical jobs, only 24 percent of the women over 35 were doing so. The less desirable jobs in service, textiles, and food processing remained available to older women workers, who had few options, further entrenching the segmentation of the female labor force.[110]

In summary, as the wartime opportunities that had allowed the increasing numbers of wage-earning women to earn unprecedented wages receded, women continued to seek work in increasing numbers but found jobs in the female-employing industries: clerical, service, and sales work. Women in the Portland-Vancouver area in 1950 were employed in similar occupations as their predecessors in the prewar period and were earning similar wages.

Glimpses of Women in the Postwar World

Alice Kessler-Harris observes that while economists and sociologists have explained "the mechanisms that lock women into place" in the segmented labor market, most analyses "leave us reaching for explanations of why women are willing that it should be so." She suggests, drawing on the work of David Montgomery and Herbert Gutman, that we examine "women as active agents in their own lives" in order to discover the role of tradition and culture both in nurturing and in discouraging resistance to the restrictions they face.[111]

In the following discussion I have selected two strands of experience in the lives of the former shipyard workers in order to explore the interaction of their shipyard experiences with postwar social, cultural, and economic realities and to illuminate the choices available to women as they attempted to shape their lives in the postwar period. The first focuses on three narrators who were supporting themselves during the postwar period and who spent some time working at Jantzen Knitting Mills, a relentlessly nonunion shop. Two of these women were among the seven narrators who supported families for several years. Although the culture of the 1940s and 1950s fostered the illusion that such cases were aberrations, between 8 and 9 percent of all families were supported by women throughout the 1940s and 1950s. While the first cluster of stories illuminates the constraints that inhibited women's resistance during the 1950s, the second cluster focuses on those women who pushed against the limits they encountered in the postwar period as they attempted to re-enter traditionally male fields of work. These six stories shed light on the dynamics of both accommodation and resistance in the postwar work force.

Edna Hopkins, who had been a pipe welder during the war, stayed home for a few years after the war and took care of her five children. She returned to work – at Jantzen Knitting Mills – in 1949. She found the work tedious and wearing, and she planned to quit when her children became self-supporting. Her plans were changed when her husband, who had been a miner, became incapacitated by silicosis, leaving Hopkins to support herself, her husband, and the two children who remained at home. "It wasn't a question of do you work or don't you," she said. "I worked. Either that or go on welfare, and I'm too proud for welfare." The Jantzen management, according to Edna Hopkins, did everything possible to keep the union out of the shop. Hopkins did not participate in any of the unsuccessful organizing drives that were conducted during the 1950s because she was afraid of losing her job.[112]

Pat Rowlands, who had been an electrician's helper in the shipyards, had not planned to work after the war was over. "I was going to be a housewife and mother," she said. "That was the thing those days." The dream of settling down with her husband and building a house was shattered in November 1945, when she was divorced ten months after the birth of her third child. Determined to support her family, she paid her mother a dollar a day to care for the children and went to work at Jantzen Knitting Mills. She was not satisfied with her job at Jantzen. "I would work so hard the clock would stand still," she remembered. Times were hard, however, and she "didn't have much choice," so she stayed at Jantzen until her mother could no longer take care of the children. Unlike Hopkins, Rowlands had preschool children, so she had to stop working. Rowlands stayed off welfare as long as she could by scrimping, saving, and raising the best vegetable garden in the neighborhood. In March 1949, Rowlands began receiving Aid to Dependent Children (ADC). She calculates that the ninety-six dollars a month she received was not much less than she cleared when she worked at Jantzen and paid her mother to care for her children. Rowlands remarried in 1950 and devoted herself to raising her children and participating in community activities. Her life illustrates the way domestic roles have often been enforced by the realities of the marketplace.[113]

Betty Niederhaus, the third narrator who worked at Jantzen, was still working there when she was interviewed. Niederhaus remained single after the war and would have liked to have continued working as a machinist because the wages and working conditions were so much better than in any of her other jobs. She worked as a clerk in a variety store until it closed and then hired on at Jantzen. After twenty-six years at Jantzen, Niederhaus finally felt she was making a decent wage when the company sold out to Wrangler, which eliminated her department and offered her a choice between minimum-wage piecework and severance pay. She stayed because she was afraid that at the age of sixty she would have difficulty finding another job.[114] Niederhaus's fears were not unfounded. Age discrimination was pervasive despite the fact that women forty-five and over composed more than one-third of the female work force in 1950 and their numbers were increasing more rapidly than any other segment of the work force.[115] Advertisements for clerical workers and telephone operators often specified young women, while those for power machine operators in textile mills pointed out that "elderly ladies" were accepted.[116]

"Men get a bigger break," commented Niederhaus.

Why should the men's jobs pay so much more than a woman's? We exert ourselves just as much as they do. I'm down there working as fast as I can with my hands and every minute looking at the clock and I'm getting $3.25 an hour. I go in there to get my car fixed and I see on the wall he's getting 28 dollars an hour. And they're standing around talking . . . and he's getting 28 dollars an hour! . . . The men, they can work, pay the bills, and even have a little savings on the side, where a woman struggles, struggles, struggles and works just as hard, maybe sometimes even harder than some of the men, and . . . can't make ends meet. . . . And the work that they do is just as important as some of the men's work. The men automatically get more pay because they figure he's got a family. But then a single man still gets paid whether he has a family or not, but a single woman's . . . not going to get paid as much. Why a single man needs more than a single woman, I don't know. . . . They just draw a line. In the shipyards they didn't draw a line. They needed the woman's help. . . . 'We'll pay you men's wages to do a man's job because we need your help' – then it was okay.[117]

Sherna Gluck has suggested that the changed consciousness of women war workers "contributed to the tide of rising expectations for women."[18] In some ways, this was true for these three women. Shipyard work was the most satisfying work any of them had done and, as Betty Niederhaus's comments illustrate, it heightened their awareness of inequality in the postwar work force. But raised expectations involve not only an awareness of inequality and a belief in one's rights, but also some sense of choice and possibility. None of these women felt that they had much choice in their lives. The low wages available to them allowed them no margin to look for other jobs, get additional training, or participate in union efforts that might endanger their positions. And most important, there was no political movement that could offer either support or vision.

Pulling Their Own Strings

There were some women who did attempt to challenge the barriers between male and female work. Although several other narrators mentioned that they would have liked to have continued using the skills they'd acquired during the war, three of the women we interviewed, Nona Pool, Reva Baker, and Katherine Baker, attempted to do so in the 1950s and 1960s.[119] Their efforts were unsuccessful until the late 1960s and early 1970s, when two of them gained entry into skilled crafts.

Nona Pool said of her shipyard experience, "It made an industrial worker out of me." Pool changed jobs nineteen times in attempts to find industrial work that used her mechanical ability and paid decently. She stopped working in 1959, but returned ten years later when her husband became terminally ill. When Pool's husband first became sick

> he said, "All you'll be able to get will be a babysitting job or housekeeping job, you know, after you've been off work that long." I says, "You wanna bet?" [laughs] So I got me a telephone book and I found all the small manufacturers and I asked them, "Do you manufacture your product on-site?" And I called up asking 'em, "Here I am all bright-eyed and bushy-tailed. You need me to help you do that work down there?"[120]

Pool worked at a variety of jobs, mostly poorly paid and unskilled. Sometime in the late 1950s she approached someone at Freightliner Corporation, the company that eventually hired her, and asked:

> "How about giving me a job welding?" And the guy, he turned around and looked at me and he kind of laughed and he says, "I wouldn't doubt you're a good welder, but we don't have facilities for women." I said, "I'll bring my own potty; just bring me a curtain." And he laughed about that, and you know when I did finally go down there he remembered me. He kidded me about that.[121]

Pool saw herself as a "go-getter": persistent, resourceful and good-humored. While she maintained her desire to return to welding throughout this period, she at no time pursued organizational solutions. She had no hope that the union would help her, since her shipyard experience had convinced her that it protected male privilege. She knew of no other organizations or legislation; the 1950s was not a period in which women thought of collective strategies. Like most women, Pool's approach to her problems was an individual one. Her individual perseverance did, however, eventually converge with legal and social changes that loosened restrictions against women welders. In the late 1960s she got a job building radiators at Freightliner and she "kept asking them to go to welding and one of the guys said, 'Well, over my dead body will you get to be a welder.' So I went to welding school again at the community college." When she finished her course in the early 1970s, she was hired as a welder at Freightliner and welded until her retirement in 1978.[122]

Most of the married women who entered or re-entered the work force in the 1940s and 1950s waited until their children were in school. As Pat Rowlands' story illustrates, the absence of child care could be an insurmountable obstacle for those women who wanted or needed to work. Despite scarce child-care resources, however, a growing minority of women were joining the work force while their children were under five. While the percentage of black women with preschool children who were employed remained fairly constant between 1940 and 1950 (19.9 in 1940 and 20.9 in 1950), the percentage of white mothers of young children in the work force increased from 6.5 percent in 1940 to 11.1 percent in 1950.[123]

Reva Baker was among this group of wage-earning mothers. Baker's early departure from the shipyards had been precipitated by her foreman's refusal to pay her for the inspecting work she was doing. She got married during the war, then went to work as an operator for the telephone company. When her son was born she quit to stay home until he was two and a half. She then returned to the telephone company, leaving her son first with a neighbor and then with her mother (who had moved into her community). Baker remained with the telephone company all her working life, working her way up from an operator into a variety of jobs. Like Pool, she was able to re-enter traditionally male terrain in the 1970s when she became a frame attendant, working with the wires that connect customer telephone lines to central office equipment. The job involves using hand tools, climbing ladders, and carrying sixty pounds of equipment, and she encountered some resistance when she first expressed interest. In responding to her boss's hesitation she invoked her shipyard experience. "When I first told my boss that I wanted the frame job," she remembered, "he told me I wouldn't like it because it was dirty work, and I said, 'I've done dirty work all my life, I'm not afraid of dirt.' And he says, 'You'll get so tired running up and down those ladders,' and I said, 'I've been up and down ladders before.'" Baker convinced him, and her last two jobs, both involving work with central office equipment at the telephone company, were her favorite jobs. When she retired, she arranged, over some opposition, to reproduce on her retirement notice a picture of a woman with a plow, accompanied by the caption "Back then you could pick the field of your choice." She added: "Today the field of choice requires that you pull your own strings."[124]

Katherine Baker's attempt to break through the barriers to skilled work was less successful than those of Reva Baker (her sister-in-law) or Nona Pool. Katherine Baker credits her shipyard experience with her conviction that "women did have a place in the working world, certainly, and that if old Ed Kaiser could do so well paying these women as much as he paid his men—it certainly put that kind of idea in my head." After working as a grocery clerk for many years,

Baker got a job doing office work at Precision Cast Parts. Women in the plant, according to Baker, worked either in the office or in wax molding. She noticed that they used welders in the salvage department and asked the salvage foreman if he had ever hired any women.

> He said, "No, I never heard of anyone wanted to." "Well," I said, "I've done welding before, a lot of years ago. I imagine, with a little brush-up course to get acquainted with the type of metal that you're working with, I don't see why I couldn't." He said, "I wouldn't have any objection to having a woman work here, but I don't think the manager would buy it." I spoke to him again a week or two later and he said, "Absolutely not, no way." You kind of got the feeling it was because welding paid X amount of money and women didn't get paid that kind of money.[125]

Katherine Baker complained about the sexism at Precision Cast Parts until she retired, criticizing pay differentials, the double standard for male and female performance, the exclusion of women from policy-making, and the male chauvinist attitudes of the bosses. Throughout her life she clung to the conviction that "women and men should be treated equally at work," a belief that took shape in the shipyards. "I still believe that," she said. "You don't see it very many places, but I still believe it. A job is a job and someday those same boys are gonna pay for it, one way or another – they'll pay for tramping women down under their feet." After she retired, the women in Baker's plant filed a sex discrimination suit that included her; they told her that "they never could have done it if it hadn't been for me." Katherine Baker's image of herself was as "the most famous rebel that ever worked" at Precision Cast Parts. "They're still suffering from me," she commented with pleasure.[126]

The stories of Nona Pool, Reva Baker, and Katherine Baker represent the form that female rebellion frequently took in the postwar period before the reemergence of feminism. All three women were acting as individuals: Nona Pool, resourceful and persistent, Reva Baker, assertive and determined, Katherine Baker, angry and defiant. Nona Pool captured the spirit of their approach to work: "What you've got to do is say 'I'm this wide and I'm gonna push a hole in there just the right size for me and if you don't like it that's tough stuff.'"[127] They acted in isolation without support and they left a legacy for their daughters and co-workers. (One of Nona Pool's daughters became a welder and also works for Freightliner.)

While these glimpses of the postwar lives of ex-shipyard workers certainly do not tell us what all American women wanted, valued, or experienced, they do suggest that some women's attitudes towards work were changing in the decades that followed the war resulting in a growing sense of themselves as workers. Their shipyard experience contributed to these changes, which remained submerged beneath the apparent domestic consensus of the postwar era.

These postwar histories suggest the complexity of what has been described as women's "choice" of a family-centered identity in the postwar world. Women survived as well as they could in an environment offering few options. Those who attempted to widen their range of choices fought their battles alone and without support until the 1970s.

As several scholars have shown, the wartime emergency stimulated conservative impulses in the community, which sought to preserve the traditional family and traditional notions of femininity.[128] In the Portland-Vancouver community, as in the country as a whole, the belief that the housewife-mother was the centerpiece of a well-balanced family life seemed to intensify under the pressure of wartime dislocations and anxiety.[129] The traditional division of labor in the home was often associated with order, and order was seen as a source of stability and security. The nostalgic equation of a home-centered mother with childhood health and family happiness contributed to the full-scale blossoming of the feminine mystique in the postwar period.

But behind the fluctuations of Depression, war, and the feminine mystique lay the steady increase in the number of women, particularly married women, who worked for wages. While most women married, had children and saw their roles as wives and mothers as primary, an increasing number of working-class women, for a variety of reasons, also saw themselves as workers and tried, as much as the limited opportunities allowed, to find decent-paying and satisfying work. This emerging consciousness collided with the pervasive discrimination against women in the work force, both retarding the development of new attitudes towards women and work and contributing to the tensions that were building in women's lives.

Most of the women we interviewed were interested not in careers but in jobs that would challenge them and provide some measure of economic security. Their growing sense of themselves as workers was not in contradiction to their identities as wives and mothers; it was part of their commitment to their families. Many of the women interviewed had the two-stage work lives typical of women workers during this period – re-entering the work force when their children were grown – and they encountered the frustrations of the work world in the second stage of their work lives. Of the twenty-nine narrators who worked for wages after the war, only six felt satisfied with any of their jobs after the shipyards. The experience of most of them could be described by Loena Ellis's remark, "I never did find a comfortable place to work."[130]

For women shipyard workers, World War II was a fleeting opportunity to earn recognition and decent wages at a time when increasing numbers of women were perceiving waged work and family life as compatible. As Deborah Hirschfield has shown, the employment of large numbers of women had little permanent impact on the shipbuilding industry.[131] It did, however, leave a lasting imprint on the lives of many of the women we interviewed. Berenice Thompson was worn out at the end of the war and happy to have more time at home, but she felt that she gained a sense of equality with men from working at the shipyards. She felt that she could say to her husband "who didn't think women could buy anything or own anything": . . . "I am something just as much as you are Mr. Thompson."[132] "It was a breakthrough," said Pat Koehler, "because we knew we could do things."[133] Kathryn Blair reflected, "It gave me enough courage to know I could at least speak up for myself. And I could take care of myself. . . . I think I probably learned from that experience that I could always manage."[134]

NOTES

Introduction

1. Joanne Hudlicky, interview, April 12, 1981.

2. Rosa Dickson, interview, April 2, 1981.

3. Beatrice Marshall, interview, June 11, 1981.

4. The first analysts to question this image were Lisa Anderson and Sheila Tobias in "What Really Happened to Rosie the Riveter? Demobilization and the Female Labor Force 1944-47," (New York: MSS Modular Publications, 1974). See also Paddy Quick, "Rosie the Riveter, Myths and Realities," *Radical America* 9 (July–August 1975); Alice Kessler-Harris, *Out to Work: A History of Wage-Earning Women in the United States* (New York: Oxford University Press, 1982); Karen Anderson, *Wartime Women: Sex Roles, Family Relations, and the Status of Women during World War II* (Westport, Conn.: Greenwood, 1981) and Susan Hartmann, *The Home Front and Beyond: American Women in the 1940s* (Boston: Twayne, 1982).

5. Karen Anderson, "Last Hired, First Fired: Black Women Workers during World War II," *Journal of American History* 69 (June 1982), pp. 82-97.

6. William H. Chafe, *The American Woman: Her Changing Social, Economic, and Political Role 1920-1970* (New York: Oxford University Press, 1972) Chapter 8; Eugenia Kaledin, *Mothers and More: American Women in the 1950s* (Boston: G. K. Hall, 1984) chapter 4.

7. Eleanor Straub, "Government Policy toward Civilian Women during World War II" (Ph.D. dissertation, Emory University, 1973); Josephine Chandler Holcomb, "Women in the Labor Force in the United States, 1940-1950," (Ph.D. dissertation, University of South Carolina, 1976).

8. Leila J. Rupp, *Mobilizing Women for War: German and American Propaganda, 1939-1945* (Princeton: Princeton University Press, 1978); Maureen Honey, *Creating Rosie the Riveter: Class, Gender and Propaganda during World War II* (Amherst: University of Massachusetts Press, 1984), and "The 'Womanpower' Campaign: Advertising and Recruitment Propaganda during World War II," *Frontiers* 6 (1981), pp. 51-56; Susan Hartmann,

"Prescriptions for Penelope: Literature on Women's Obligations to Returning Veterans," *Women's Studies* 5 (1978), p. 224.

9. Anderson, *Wartime Women*.

10. Karen Beck Skold, "Women Workers and Child Care During World War II: A Case Study of the Portland, Oregon, Shipyards" (Ph.D. dissertation, University of Oregon, 1981); Ruth Milkman, "Organizing the Sexual Division of Labor: Historical Perspectives on 'Women's Work' and the American Labor Movement," *Socialist Revolution* 10 (January–February 1980), and "Redefining Women's Work: The Sexual Division of Labor in the Auto Industry during World War II," *Feminist Studies* 8 (Summer 1982).

11. Milkman, "Redefining Women's Work," p. 340.

12. Holcomb, p. 177; D'Ann Campbell, *Women at War with America: Private Lives in a Patriotic Era* (Cambridge, Mass: Harvard University Press, 1984). For a useful examination of union attitudes during World War I see Maurine Weiner Greenwald, *Women, War and Work: The Impact of World War I on Women Workers in the United States* (Westport, Conn.: Greenwood, 1980), p. 242.

13. Ruth Milkman, *Gender at Work: The Dynamics of Job Segregation by Sex during World War II* (University of Illinois Press, Urbana and Chicago, 1987).

14. Andrea Walsh, *Women's Film and Female Experience 1940–1950* (New York: Praeger, 1984), pp. 15, 197.

15. Walsh, pp. 4, 26.

16. Campbell, p. 234.

17. Campbell, p. 15.

18. Alice Kessler-Harris, "Equal Employment Opportunity Commission v. Sears, Roebuck and Company: A Personal Account," *Radical History Review* 35 (April 1986), p. 68.

19. Joanne Hudlicky, interview, April 20, 1981. See Alice Kessler-Harris, above, for a fuller discussion of the interaction of opportunity and choice in relation to women wage earners.

20. Sherna Berger Gluck, *Rosie the Riveter Revisited: Women, the War and Social Change* (Boston: G. K. Hall, 1987), pp. 268.

21. Gluck, p. 265.

22. In choosing this approach I am drawing on the recent work of social psychologists such as Rhoda Unger, whose work has focused on the "interactive relationships between the person and the social environment." This work

steers a course between a strict social constructionist model in which people's behavior is shaped by their environment and a model that assumes free choice. See, for example, Rhoda Unger, "Sex, Gender and Epistemology" in M. Crawford and M. Gentry, eds., *Gender and Thought* (New York: Sprenger-Verlag, 1989).

23. Frederic C. Lane, *Ships for Victory: A History of Shipbuilding under the U.S. Maritime Commission in World War II* (Baltimore: Johns Hopkins University Press, 1951), p. 257.

24. Dorothy Newman, *Employing Women in the Shipyards* (Washington, D.C.: Government Printing Office, 1944, p. 1.

25. For a national overview of women in the shipbuilding industry during World War II see Deborah Ann Hirschfield, "Rosie Also Welded: Women and Technology in Shipbuilding during World War II," Ph.D. dissertation, University of California at Irvine, 1987.

26. Lane, p. 257; *The Oregonian*, April 27, 1944.

27. E. Kimbark MacColl, *Growth of a City: Power and Politics in Portland, Oregon 1915–1950* (Portland: Georgian, 1979), p. 606.

28. For a national overview of child care during the war and a discussion of its problems see Anderson, *Wartime Women* chapter 4; Hartmann, *The Home Front and Beyond*, pp. 58–59; Richard Polenberg, *War and Society: The United States 1941–45* (Philadelphia: Lippincott, 1972), pp. 148–49.

29. Frankie Cooper was the only narrator who was not living in the Portland-Vancouver area. Her interview was conducted by a member of the Rosie the Riveter Project from San Francisco. The oral history tapes have been deposited in the Oregon Historical Society. "Good Work, Sister! Women Shipyard Workers of World War II: An Oral History," the slide-tape show based on the interviews, was completed in March 1982. For a description of the project see Amy Kesselman, Karen Wickre, and Tina Tau, "Good Work, Sister! The Making of an Oral History Production," *Frontiers* 7 (1983), pp. 64–70. "Good Work, Sister!" is available for rental or purchase in videotape and slide-tape format from the Northwest Women's History Project, P.O. Box 5692, Portland, OR 97228.

30. Sherna Berger Gluck, "Women's Oral History, the Second Decade," *Frontiers: A Journal of Women's Studies* 7 (1983), pp. 1–2; Mary Aicken Rothchild, "Using Oral History to Find the 'Common Women': An Arizona Oral History Project," *Frontiers: A Journal of Women's Studies* 7 (1983), pp. 87–90. Mary E. Pidgeon, *Changes in Women's Employment during the War*, Special Bulletin No. 20 (Washington, D.C.: Government Printing Office, 1944), p. 29; June Herzog, "Study of the Negro Defense Worker in the Portland-Vancouver Area," senior thesis, Reed College, 1944, p. 77; *The People's Observer*, March 31, 1945.

31. We interviewed three black women and ten women who were in their late thirties and early forties during the war, but were unable to achieve the 23.5 percent who were over forty-five during the war since there were few women in that age group available for interviews.

32. Thirty-six women were interviewed; one interview included two women. All of the narrators had been production workers except Betty Cleator, who was a draftsman.

33. "Movement without Aim: Methodological and Theoretical Problems in Oral History," in Ron J. Grele, ed., *Envelopes of Sound: Six Practitioners Discuss the Method, Theory and Practice of Oral History and Oral Testimony* (Chicago: Precedent, 1975), p. 137.

34. Honey, "The 'Womanpower' Campaign," p. 5.

35. Grele, p. 235.

36. Ruth Drurey, interview, April 18, 1981.

37. Jesse Lemisch, "Is a Diary a Primary Source? 'Eyewitness Testimony,' Exponential Decay, and Back Transforms; or Some Good News and Bad News from Modern Brain Research with Reference to the Historian's Use of Reminiscences," paper presented at meeting of the Organization of American Historians, Los Angeles, California, April 1984, p. 5.

38. For a related discussion of what they call "social amnesia born of defeat and the failure of trade unionism to take root in a living tradition" among the people they interviewed for their study of cotton mill workers, see Jacqueline Dowd Hall et al., *Like a Family: The Making of a Southern Cotton Mill World* (Chapel Hill: University of North Carolina Press, 1987) p. xv.

Chapter 1

1. U.S. Congress, House Committee on Naval Affairs, *Hearings on Congested Areas*, 1944, 78th Congress, 2nd session, p. 1275; Portland Area Postwar Development Committee, William Bowes Papers, Box 14, Oregon Historical Society (hereafter cited as OHS).

2. Forest Rieke, interview with Karen Skold January 9, 1976, transcript. Part 2, p. 8, Karen Skold Interviews, OHS.

3. *Who's Who in Finance and Industry*, 22nd edition (Chicago: Marquis, 1981), p. 340; *Who's Who in America*, vol. 24 (Chicago: Marquis, 1946), p. 1304. See Frederic C. Lane, *Ships for Victory: A History of Shipbuilding under the United States Maritime Commission in World War II* (Baltimore: Johns Hopkins University Press, 1951), p. 54, for a description of Henry Kaiser's involvement with the World War II shipbuilding program. For Kaiser Corporation's profits from wartime shipbuilding, see *Hearings*, U.S. House of Representatives, Subcommittee on Shipyard Profits of the Committee on

Merchant Marine and Fisheries, 78th Cong., March 22 and 23, 1944, and Lane, pp. 811–18.

4. Lane, *Ships for Victory*, pp. 54–55, 146.

5. *Commerce*, December 5, 1942.

6. Elijah Baker, *Introduction to Steel Shipbuilding* (New York: McGraw Hill, 1953) p. xvi.

7. "Kaiser Shipbuilding during the War," p. 2, Kaiser Historical Library.

8. Deborah Ann Hirschfield, "Rosie Also Welded: Women and Technology in Shipbuilding during World War II" (Ph.D. dissertation, University of California at Irvine, 1987), pp. 76–89.

9. George Smith to Philip Van Gelder, November 19, 1941, Papers of the Industrial Union of Marine and Shipbuilding Workers of America (IUMSWA), Box 211, University of Maryland.

10. *Commerce*, August 1, 1942; *The Columbian*, September 28, 1943.

11. A memo from Henry Kaiser to Admiral Vickery reported that Kaiser decided to recruit workers from outside the Portland-Vancouver area in August 1942 and that between August 1942 and June 1943 an average of 3,000 workers a month were recruited. Henry Kaiser to Admiral Howard L. Vickery, June 14, 1943, U.S. Maritime Commission Records, RG 178, Box 415, National Archives Suitland, Maryland.

12. *The Columbian*, September 22, 1942. For a history of Vanport see Manly Maben, *Vanport* (Portland: Oregon Historical Society, 1987).

13. *The Shipbuilder*, June 24, 1942 and July 10, 1942.

14. Dorothy Newman, *Employing Women in the Shipyards* (Washington, D.C.: U.S. Department of Labor, 1944), pp. 1–3.

15. *The Oregonian*, November 9, 1941.

16. *Bo's'n's Whistle*, March 26, 1942.

17. *The Oregonian*, February 8, 1942; Durward Howes, ed., *American Women: The Standard Biographical Dictionary of American Women*, vol. 3 (Los Angeles: American, 1939).

18. Oregon Division of Vocational Education, *Descriptive Report of Vocational Training for War Production Workers*, (Salem, Oregon, June 1945), p. 3.

19. *Descriptive Report*, p. 3.

20. *The Oregonian*, May 21, 1942.

21. Lane, *Ships for Victory*, 238–258; Augusta Clawson, "Report on Welding Training and Shipyard Employment," April 1943, p. 6, Office of Education Records, R.G. 12, National Archives.

22. *Descriptive Report*, p. 15.

23. *The Oregonian*, "The Daily Home Magazine," May 21, 1942, p. 3.

24. *Master Agreement Covering New Ship Construction Between Oregon Shipbuilding Corporation and The Metal Trades Council of Portland and Vicinity*, May 12, 1941.

25. "Charges against Oregon Shipbuilding Corporation," November 4, 1941; Phillip Van Gelder to John Green, November 30, 1942, Papers of the Industrial Union of Marine and Shipbuilding Workers of America (IUMSWA), Box 211, Special Collections, University of Maryland. This collection includes many documents relating to this case, which, in addition to the jurisdictional dispute, raised the questions of AFL racketeering, lack of democracy in the Metal Trade Unions, discrimination against black workers, and excessive initiation fees. *New York Times*, November 30, 1942; *The Columbian*, May 26, June 2, June 3, and June 8, 1943.

26. See Elizabeth Gurley Flynn, *Women in the War* (New York: Workers Library, 1942), p. 16, for a description of the demonstration by workers at Marin Shipyards in Sausalito.

27. *The Boilermakers Journal*, August 1942, p. 230.

28. *The Shipbuilder*, August 21, 1942.

29. *The Shipbuilder*, August 21, 1942.

30. For discussion of opposition to admitting women in the Seattle Boilermakers local see Karen Anderson, *Wartime Women: Sex Roles, Family Relations, and the Status of Women during World War II* (Westport, Conn.: Greenwood, 1981), p. 43.

31. *The Boilermakers Journal*, October 1942, p. 292.

32. *The Shipbuilder*, September 11, 1942, p. 7.

33. *Commerce*, October 17, 1942.

34. *The Boilermakers' Journal*, October 1942, p. 319.

35. *Stem to Stern*, September 1943; U.S. Employment Service (USES) Labor Market Reports, Records of the War Manpower Commission, RG 183, Box 26, National Archives (hereafter cited as N.A.); Field Report, Margaret Kay Anderson, August 8, 1943, Eleanor Bradley to Margaret Anderson, March 1943, Women's Bureau Papers, U.S. Department of Labor, RG 86, Box 1413, N.A.

36. International Labor Office, *The War and Women's Employment: The Experience of the United Kingdom and the United States* (Montreal: International Labour Office, 1946), p. 143.

37. *The Oregonian*, December 4, 1942 and February 14, 1943.

38. *The Oregonian*, February 14, 1943 and April 18, 1943.

39. *The Oregonian*, June 20, 1943; War Manpower Commission, *Survey of Shipyard Operations in the Portland, Oregon Metropolitan Area*, vol. 2, p. 72.

40. War Manpower Commission, *Survey*, vol. 3, p. 30.

41. U.S. Department of the Census, 16th Decennial Census, vol. 2, Part 5, p. 953.

42. Margaret Kay Anderson to Mary Anderson, February 4, 1943, Women's Bureau Records RG 86, Box 1413, N.A.

43. Sara Southall and Thelma McKelvey, Report, May 20, 1943, U.S. Maritime Commission Records, RG 178, Box 415, N.A.

44. LueRayne Culbertson, interview, May 4, 1981.

45. Edgar Kaiser to Admiral Vickery, June 14, 1943, U.S. Maritime Commission Records, RG 178, Box 415, NA.

46. *The Oregonian*, June 20, 1943.

47. *The Oregonian*, June 18, 1943.

48. Berenice Thompson, interview, November 20, 1980.

49. *The Oregonian*, April 27, 1944.

50. Moses Plan, City Planning Files, Box 20, Portland City Archives (hereafter cited as PCA).

51. "Women War Workers and Recent Economic Change," *Monthly Labor Review*, December 1947, p. 667; Portland Committe on Postwar Planning, Shipyard Survey, Planning Files, Box 20, PCA.

52. The survey questioned 91,036 workers altogether and included both men and women. The prewar occupations table is not broken down by sex, but I'm assuming all workers who described themselves as housewives were women. Portland Committee on Postwar Planning, Shipyard Survey, Summary Table, p. 4, Planning Files, Box 20, PCA. See chapter 6 for more detail on this survey.

53. U.S. Department of Labor, Women's Bureau, *Changes in Women's Employment during the War* (Washington, D.C.: 1944), Government Printing Office, pp. 2–3.

54. Shipyard Survey, Summary Tables, p. 4. In 1981 The Northwest Women's History Project conducted a telephone survey with 157 women who had worked at skilled trades in Portland and Vancouver during the war. The telephone survey asked, "What work were you doing before working in the shipyards?" Thirty-two percent said they were housewives.

55. Alice Kessler-Harris, *Out to Work: A History of Wage-Earning Women in the United States* (New York: Oxford University Press, 1982), p. 278.

56. Alice Kessler Harris, "Independence and Virtue in the Lives of Wage-Earning Women, the U.S., 1870–1930," in *Women in Culture and Politics*, ed. Judith Friedlander, Blanche Wiesen Cook, Alice Kessler-Harris, and Carroll Smith-Rosenberg (Bloomington: Indiana University Press, 1986), p. 15.

57. Quoted in Lois Sharf, *To Work and to Wed: Female Employment, Feminism and the Great Depression* (Westport, Conn.: Greenwood, 1980) quotes on pp. 50, 107.

58. Etta Harvey, interview, May 28, 1981.

59. Marie Merchant, interview, July 20, 1981; Jacqueline Jones, *Labor of Love, Labor of Sorrow: Black Women, Work and the Family from Slavery to the Present* (New York: Random House, 1985), p. 205.

60. Dorothy Anderson, interview, May 22, 1981; Ruth Drurey, interview, April 18, 1981; and Betty Cleator, interview, June 6, 1981.

61. See, for example, Christine Bose, "Household Resources and U.S. Women's Work: Factors Affecting Gainful Employment at the Turn of the Century," *American Sociological Review* 49 (August 1984), pp. 474–90.

62. Alice Erickson, interview, June 5, 1981.

63. Audrey Moore, interview, June 15, 1981.

64. Pat Rowlands, interview, May 20, 1981.

65. Nell Conley, interview, April 3, 1981.

66. Valerie Kincade Oppenheimer, *The Female Labor Force in the United States: Demographic and Economic Factors Governing Its Growth and Changing Composition* (Berkeley: Institute of International Studies, 1970), p. 130; Ree Adkins, interview, June 2, 1981.

67. Jeanne Westin, *Making Do: How Women Survived the Thirties* (New York: Follett, 1976).

68. Nona Pool, interview, May 25, 1981; Billie Strmiska, interview, June 14, 1981; and Beatrice Hadley, interview, June 5, 1981.

69. Nona Pool, interview, May 25, 1981.

70. Billie Strimska, interview, June 4, 1981.

71. Beatrice Hadley, interview, June 5, 1981.

72. Helen Berggren, interview, May 23, 1981.

73. Rosa Dickson, interview, April 2, 1981.

74. See Veronica Beechey, *Unequal Work* (London: Verso, 1987), and Kessler-Harris in *Out to Work* for the argument that women's home and market labor should be seen as a "continuum."

75. Nona Pool, interview, May 25, 1981.

76. Lois Housman, interview, May 22, 1981.

77. Patricia Koehler, interview, June 6, 1981.

78. Virginia Larson, interview, April 12, 1981.

79. Rosa Dickson, interview, April 2, 1981.

80. Doris Avshalomov, interview, June 5, 1981.

81. Nell Conley, interview, April 3, 1981.

82. Kathryn Blair, interview, April 26, 1981.

83. International Labour Office, *The War and Women's Employment: The Experience of the United Kingdom and the United States* (Montreal: International Labour Office, 1946), p. 209.

84. Betty Cleator, interview, June 6, 1981.

85. Jean Clark, interview, June 2, 1981.

86. Etta Harvey, interview, May 28, 1981.

87. Berenice Thompson, interview, November 20, 1980

88. Loena Ellis, interview, May 15, 1981.

Chapter Two

1. *Flat Top Flash*, November 13, 1943. Maureen Honey, in *Creating Rosie the Riveter: Class, Gender and Propaganda during World War II* (Amherst: University of Massachusetts Press, 1984), chapter 1, demonstrates that this spirit pervaded the national propaganda used to mobilize women workers.

2. For a national survey of women in shipyard work see Deborah Ann Hirschfield, "Rosie Also Welded: Women and Technology in Shipbuilding dur-

ing World War II" (Ph.D. dissertation, University of California at Irvine, 1987); Mary Martha Thomas comments that the shipyards in Mobile, Alabama, hired women only after pressure from the WMC and the USES in *Riveting and Rationing in Dixie: Alabama Women and the Second World War* (Tuscaloosa: University of Alabama Press, 1987), p. 42.

3. U.S. War Manpower Commission, *Survey of Shipyard Operations in the Portland, Oregon, Metropolitan Area,* Portland, Oregon: U.S. War Manpower Commission, 1943, Vol. II, p. 32.

4. Dorothy Newman, *Employing Women in the Shipyards* (Washington, D.C.: Government Printing Office, 1944), p. 3.

5. Karen Beck Skold, "Women Workers and Child Care during World War II: A Case Study of the Portland, Oregon, Shipyards" (Ph.D. dissertation, University of Oregon, 1981), p. 92; see Chapter 3 for a full discussion of sex segregation in the Kaiser shipyards.

6. Lois Housman, interview, May 22, 1981.

7. Ruth Milkman, "Redefining 'Women's Work': The Sexual Division of Labor in the Auto Industry during World War II," *Feminist Studies* 8 (Summer) 1981), quote on p. 340. See also p. 345, 353 and Milkman, *Gender at Work: The Dynamics of Job Segregation by Sex during World War II* (Urbana: University of Illinois Press, 1987) chapter 4.

8. *The Boilermakers Journal,* October 1943, p. 292.

9. Newman, p. 22.

10. Newman, p. 28.

11. Margaret Kay Anderson to Mary Anderson, June 4, 1943, U.S. Department of Labor, Women's Bureau Papers, RG 86, Box 1413, National Archives (hereafter cited as NA).

12. Newman, p. 21.

13. Bertha Nienberg to Margaret Kay Anderson, April 16, 1943, Women's Bureau Papers, Box 1413. For a discussion of the relationship between the Women's Bureau and other federal agencies involved in the recruitment of female labor during the war see Judith Sealander, *As Minority Becomes Majority: Federal Reaction to the Phenomenon of Women in the Work Force, 1920–1963* (Westport, Conn.: Greenwood, 1983), pp. 100–102.

14. Margaret Kay Anderson to Mary Anderson, Women's Bureau Papers, Box 1413.

15. Sara Southall and Thelma McKelvey, "A Suggested Program of Plant Utilization of Women Workers in the Kaiser Shipbuilding Corporation Yards," May 20, 1943, U.S. Maritime Commission Records, RG 178, Box 415,

NA; Margaret Kay Anderson to Mary Anderson, May 27, 1943, Women's Bureau Papers, Box 1413.

16. Margaret Kay Anderson to Mary Anderson, May 18, 1943, Women's Bureau Papers, Box 1413. This letter includes a report on a meeting with Ann Treadwell after she returned from Portland.

17. Newman, p. 28.

18. *Bo's'n's Whistle*, May 20, 1943.

19. *Oregon Journal*, October 5, 1944.

20. *Bo's'n's Whistle*, May 20, 1943.

21. U.S. War Manpower Commission (hereafter cited as WMC), *Survey of Shipyard Operations in the Portland Metropolitan Area*, vol. 3, p. 37.

22. Doris Avshalomov, interview, June 5, 1981.

23. Mabel Davis (Hegg), interview, May 15, 1981.

24. Reva Baker, interview, April 24, 1981.

25. Hirshfield, "Rosie," Chapter 1.

26. Frederic C. Lane, *Ships for Victory: A History of Shipbuilding under the United States Maritime Commission in World War II* (Baltimore: Johns Hopkins University Press, 1951), chapter 8.

27. Newman, p. 28.

28. Reva Baker, interview, April 24, 1981.

29. Newman, p. 33.

30. Edna Hopkins, interview, May 28, 1981.

31. Beatrice Hadley, interview, June 5, 1981.

32. Quoted in Thomas, *Riveting and Rationing in Dixie*, p. 45.

33. William Harris, "Federal Intervention in Union Discrimination: The Fair Employment Practices Commission and West Coast Shipyards during World War II," (unpublished paper, Indiana University, 1978); Margaret Kay Anderson, report on interview with Edwin Berry of the Portland Urban League, November 19, 1946, Women's Bureau Papers; *The People's Observer*, March 31, 1945; June Herzog, "Study of the Negro Defense Worker in the Portland-Vancouver Area," (senior thesis, Reed College, 1944); *The Columbian*, December 14, 1943.

34. "Miscellaneous Negro Personnel Data"; *Anderson et al. v. Oregon Shipbuilding Corporation, Kaiser Vancouver, Kaiser Swan Island, and the In-*

ternational Brotherhood of Boilermakers, Iron Shipbuilders, Blacksmiths, Forgers and Helpers, Selected Documents of the Records of the Committee on Fair Employment Practice (hereafter cited as FEPC), roll #13, microfilm; Herzog, p. 30.

35. Audrey Moore, June 15, 1981, Doris Avshalamov, June 5, 1981; Mabel Davis (Hegg), May 15, 1981; Marie Merchant, July 20, 1981; Beatrice Marshall, June 11, 1981: interviews.

36. WMC, *Survey,* vol. 3, p. 52. "Miscellaneous Negro Personnel Data," U.S. Fair Employment Practices Committee, roll #13, microfilm.

37. Testimony of Virginia Lemire, Hearings, November 1943, Records of the FEPC, roll #13, microfilm.

38. "NYA Trains Shipyard Workers," *Marine Engineering and Shipping Review,* February 1942.

39. Beatrice Marshall, interview, June 11, 1981.

40. Herzog, p. 63.

41. Beatrice Marshall, interview, June 11, 1981.

42. "Final Disposition Report," Case #12-BR-339, Records of the FEPC, Region 12, roll #110, microfilm.

43. Lee Stoll to Harry Klingman, April 26, Records of the FEPC, roll #110, microfilm.

44. "Final Disposition Report," Case #12-BR-339.

45. Doris Mae Williams to the FEPC, August 14, 1944, FEPC, roll #110, microfilm.

46. "Final Disposition Report," Case #12-BR-339.

47. *The People's Observer,* June 30, 1944.

48. Beatrice Marshall, interview, June 11, 1981.

49. Virginia Larson, interviews, April 12, 1981; Loena Ellis, interviews, May 15, 1981.

50. Reva Baker, interview, April 24, 1981.

51. Joanne Hudlicky, interview, April 20, 1981; LueRayne Culbertson, interview, May 4, 1981.

52. Joanne Hudlicky, interview, April 20, 1981.

53. Ibid.

54. Alice Erickson, interview, June 5, 1981.

55. *Bo's'n's Whistle*, August 8, 1943.

56. Frankie Cooper, interview, May 20, 1981.

57. Etta Harvey, interview, May 28, 1981.

58. Augusta Clawson, Report, "Vocational Training for Production Workers," p. 8, April 1943, Office of Education Records, RG 12, NA.

59. Maude Withers, "Women in Industry," Women's Bureau Papers.

60. Audrey Moore, interview, June 15, 1981.

61. Nona Pool, interview, May 25, 1981.

62. Nell Conley, interview, April 3, 1981.

63. Berenice Thompson, interview, November 20, 1980.

64. Loena Ellis, interview, May 15, 1981.

65. Joanne Hudlicky, interview, April 20, 1981.

66. Virginia Larson, interview, April 12, 1981.

67. LueRayne Culbertson, interview, May 4, 1981.

68. Reva Baker, interview, April 24, 1981.

69. *Bo's'n's Whistle*, November 17, 1944.

70. Loena Ellis, interview, May 15, 1981.

71. *Bo's'n's Whistle* 1941–46, *The Porthole* 1944–45, *Stem to Stern* 1942–45, passim.

72. *Stem to Stern*, October 7, 1943 and July 29, 1943.

73. Katherine Archibald, *Wartime Shipyards: A Study in Social Disunity* (Berkeley: University of California Press, 1947), p. 18.

74. *Bo's'n's Whistle*, June 13, 1943, May 11, 1945, July 6, 1945; *Bo's'n's Whistle*, March 31, 1944, July 14, 1944, July 28, 1944 and August 11, 1944, December 22, 1944.

75. *Bo's'n's Whistle*, December 22, 1944.

76. *The Oregonian*, April 27, 1944, p. 2; the observations about language are based on a reading of all shipyard newspapers, *The Shipbuilder, The Oregonian*, and *The Columbian*.

77. *Bo's'n's Whistle*, September 29, 1944.

78. *The Oregonian*, September 13, 1943.

79. Lin Farley, *Sexual Shakedown: Sexual Harassment of Women on the Job* (New York: McGraw Hill, 1978), p. 13.

80. Doris Avshalomov, interview, June 5, 1981.

81. Ibid.

82. *The Columbian*, October 11, 1941. See Leila J. Rupp, *Mobilizing Women for War: German and American Propaganda, 1939–1945* (Princeton, N.J.: Princeton University Press, 1978), for a discussion of this phenomenon on a national level.

83. Nell Conley, interview, April 3, 1981.

84. *Bo's'n's Whistle*, November 26, 1942. There was concern in government circles about women wearing unsafe or cumbersome clothing. When Sara Southall and Thelma McKelvey visited the yards in June of the following year they reported that women were wearing inadequate work clothes, but were informed that government and industry were working on the problem. Southall and McKelvey, "A Suggested Program of Plant Utilization of Women Workers in the Kaiser Shipbuilding Corporation Yards," p. 7.

85. George Hutton, Industrial Safety Society, to Margaret Kay Anderson, August 13, 1943, Women's Bureau Papers.

86. *Bo's'n's Whistle*, March 24, 1944.

87. Etta Harvey, interview, May 28, 1981.

88. *Business Week*, October 17, 1942.

89. Clarence Williams to President Franklin D. Roosevelt, January 4, 1944, FEPC, roll #110, microfilm. Williams brought his case to an appeal board, which reinstated him, but to the outfitting dock, which he felt was harmful to his health.

90. Testimony of Elmer Hann, November 1943, West Coast Hearings, FEPC, roll #13, microfilm.

91. Manly, Maben, *Vanport* (Portland: Oregon Historical Society, 1987), p. 89. Black residents of Vanport were concentrated in certain sections within Vanport. Maben, pp. 92–94.

92. Doris Avshalomov, interview, June 5, 1981.

93. *Business Week*, October 17, 1942.

94. Ibid.

95. Betty Cleator, interview, June 6, 1981.

96. Newman, p. 26.

97. Doris Avshalomov, interview, June 5, 1981.

98. Jean Clark, interview, June 2, 1981.

99. Farley, p. 48.

100. Mabel Studebaker, interview, April 15, 1981.

101. Kathryn Blair, interview, April 26, 1981.

102. Lois Housman, interview, May 22, 1981.

103. LueRayne Culbertson, interview, May 4, 1981.

104. Doris Avshalomov, interview, June 5, 1981.

105. Loena Ellis, interview, May 15, 1981.

Chapter Three

1. *Stem to Stern*, August 12, 1943.

2. *Stem to Stern*, December 2, 1943.

3. See Karen Anderson, *Wartime Women: Sex Roles, Family Relations, and the Status of Women during World War II* (Westport, Conn.: Greenwood, 1981), chapter 4, for a discussion of child care in Detroit, Baltimore, and Seattle. See Sheila Tropp Lichtman, "Women at Work," 1941–1945: Wartime Employment in the San Francisco Bay Area," Ph.D. dissertation, University of California at Davis, 1981), and Susan Hartmann, *The Home Front and Beyond: American Women in the 1940s* (Boston: G. K. Hall, 1982), chapter 5, for a general discussion.

4. *Bo's'n's Whistle*, Swan Island, April 21, 1944. Contemporary studies have shown that the amount of time married women spend on housework decreases only slightly when they are employed outside the home. See, for example, Heidi Hartmann, "The Family as the Locus of Gender, Class and Political Struggle: The Example of Housework," *Signs* 6 (Spring 1981) 366–94; see Bettina Berch, *The Endless Day: The Political Economy of Women and Work* (New York: Harcourt Brace Jovanovich, 1982), for a summary of these studies.

5. Augusta Clawson, *Shipyard Diary of a Woman Welder* (New York: Penguin, 1944), p. 15.

6. LueRayne Culbertson, interview, May 4, 1981.

7. Emma Ward to Virginia Lemire, April 4, 1944, Records of the U.S. Maritime Commission, RG 178, Box 415, National Archives (hereafter cited as NA).

8. Bryn Mawr College, Carola Woerishoffer Graduate Department of Social Economy and Social Research, *Women during the War and After: A Summary of a Comprehensive Study* (New York: Curtis, 1945), p. 42.

9. Manly Maben, *Vanport*, (Portland: Oregon Historical Society Press, 1987), pp. 10, 16, 22, 25. See U.S. Congress, House Committee on Naval Affairs, "A Report of the Congested Areas Subcommittee," 78th Congress, 1st Session, November 3, 1943, pp. 1640–46 for a discussion of the stoves.

10. *Bo's'n's Whistle*, March 24, 1944; September 1, 1944. According to the Bryn Mawr study, two-thirds of one thousand stores across the country had evening hours (Bryn Mawr College, p. 54).

11. Mabel Studebaker, interview, April 15, 1981.

12. Minutes, Advisory Committee on Child Care, Health and Welfare (Oregon Child Care Committee), November 10, 1943, Papers of the Oregon State Defense Council, Oregon State Archives (hereafter cited as OSA).

13. Mary Alice Webb to Mary Anderson, May 15, 1944, Women's Bureau Papers, U.S. Department of Labor, RG 86, Box 1413, N.A.

14. U.S. War Manpower Commission, "Policy on Employment in Industry of Women with Young Children," August 15, 1942 Papers of the Oregon Defense Council, OSA.

15. Eleanor Bradley to Margaret Kay Anderson, March 19, 1943, Women's Bureau Papers, Box 1413.

16. *The Oregonian*, April 4, 1943.

17. Various titles appear on the documents of both committees. For simplicity, the Oregon Child Care Committee and the Multnomah County Day Care Committee will be used throughout this book. Minutes, Oregon Child Care Committee, OSA; Minutes of the Multnomah County Day Care Committee, Records of the Portland Council of Social Agencies, Tri-County Community Council (hereafter cited as TCCC) Papers, MSS 1783, Oregon Historical Society (hereafter cited as OHS).

18. Report, Multnomah County Day Care Committee, November 16, 1942, p. 5, Records of the Portland Council of Social Agencies, TCCC Records, MSS 1783. In an interview conducted by Karen Skold in 1976, Elizabeth Goddard, Executive Secretary of the Multnomah County Day Care Committee, described two points of view on the committee – one supporting and the other opposing group care for preschool children. The records of the committee seem to indicate that in its early days, the opposition was dominant. (Elizabeth Goddard, interview with Karen Skold, transcript, OHS).

19. Report, Oregon Child Care Committee, December 12, 1942, Papers of the Oregon State Defense Council.

20. *The Oregonian*, April 4, 1943.

21. *Bo's'n's Whistle*, March 25, 1943.

22. Anderson, *Wartime Women*, p. 51.

23. *The Oregonian*, February 14, 1943; *Bo's'n's Whistle*, October 7, 1943; U.S. War Manpower Commission, *Survey of Shipyard Operations in the Portland, Oregon, Metropolitan Area*, Vol. 2 (Portland, Oreg.: 1943), p. 53.

24. Theresa Janes, Personnel Department of Oregon Shipbuilding Corporation, "Report on Absenteeism," January 29, 1943, Records of the Portland Council of Social Agencies, TCCC Records, MSS 1783.

25. Multnomah County Day Care Committee, Report, November 16, 1942, p. 6, Records of the Portland Council of Social Agencies, TCCC Records, MSS 1783.

26. Nona Pool, interview, May 25, 1981.

27. Edna Hopkins, interview, May 28, 1981.

28. Rosa Dickson, interview, April 2, 1981.

29. Audrey Moore, interview, June 15, 1981.

30. Marie Merchant, interview, July 20.

31. Etta Harvey, interview, May 28, 1981.

32. See for example, Sheila Tropp Lichtman, "Women at Work," pp. 316–17.

33. Anderson, *Wartime Women*, chapter 4.

34. Skold, "Women Workers and Child Care during World War II: A Case Study of the Portland, Oregon Shipyards." (Ph.D. dissertation, University of Oregon, 1981) p. 165.

35. For the effect of the Kaiser centers on Lanham Act centers see transcripts of the following interviews by Karen Skold: Cornella Novak, coordinator of the public school nurseries June 12, 1976, Elizabeth Goddard, Secretary of the Multnomah County Day Care Committee May 15, 1976, and Interview #19 (teacher at a Lanham Act Child Care Center, n.d., OHS).

36. See Anderson, *Wartime Women*, p. 123, and William H. Chafe, *The American Woman: Her Changing Social, Economic, and Political Role, 1920–1970* (New York: Oxford University Press, 1972), pp. 166–170, for a discussion of the bureaucratic problems involved in the administration of Lanham Act Funds.

37. Multnomah County Day Care Committee, Report, November 25, 1942, p. 1, TCCC Records, MSS 1783.

38. "History of Oregon State Advisory Committee on Child Care, Health and Welfare," Correspondence of Governor John Hall, RG 47, OSA; Diary of Saidie Dunbar, Saidie Dunbar Papers, Ax 26, University of Oregon Library (hereafter cited as U. of O.).

39. Goddard, interview with Skold, May 15, 1976, transcript p. 26.

40. Minutes, Oregon Child Care Committee, December 19, 1942, Papers of the Oregon State Defense Council.

41. Minutes, Oregon Committee on Child Care, December 29, 1942, interview with Goddard, Skold May 15, 1976, transcript; *The Oregon Journal,* December 31, 1942.

42. Minutes, Oregon Child Care Committee, Papers of the Oregon State Defense Council; Minutes, Multnomah County Day Care Committee.

43. Minutes, Oregon Child Care Committee, March 10, 1943, Papers of the Oregon State Defense Council.

44. Eleanor Roosevelt to Admiral Land, June 9, 1943, Eleanor Roosevelt Papers, Franklin Delano Roosevelt Library.

45. Minutes, Interstate Committee on Day Care, July 19, 1943, Papers of the Oregon State Defense Council; Minutes, Oregon Day Care Committee, May 12, May 26, and August 4, 1943, Papers of the Oregon State Defense Council.

46. Mrs. C. W. Walls to Saidie Dunbar, May 11, 1943, Papers of the Oregon State Defense Council; Minutes, Oregon Child Care Committee, Papers of the Oregon Defense Council May 26, 1943; Minutes, Multnomah County Day Care Committee, September 2, 1943 TCCC Records; *The Columbian,* June 29, 1943.

47. Hazel Fredericksen, "The Program for Day Care of Children of Employed Mothers," *Social Service Review* 17 (June 1943), p. 163.

48. Fredericksen, p. 163.

49. Saidie Dunbar to Jerold Owen, May 22, 1943, Papers of the Oregon State Defense Council.

50. Minutes, Oregon Child Care Committee, August 4, 1943.

51. Ibid.

52. *The New York Times,* October 31, 1943.

53. *The Columbian,* August 16, 1943. Elizabeth Goddard, in her interview with Karen Skold, confirmed that the public schools in Vancouver were much less resistant to providing child care for employed mothers. Goddard, interview with Skold, transcript.

54. Minutes, Multnomah County Day Care Committee, September 2, 1943; Goddard, interview with Skold, transcript; Skold, "Women Workers and Childcare", chapter 4.

55. James Hymes, Jr., "The Kaiser Child Service Centers, An Interview with Lois Meek Stolz," in *Living History Interviews*, Book 2 (Carmel, Calif.: Hacienda, 1978), pp. 40, 44.

56. Hymes, p. 46.

57. Hymes, p. 43.

58. The Kaiser Company, Inc., *Child Service Centers* (Portland, Oreg., 1945).

59. Lois Meek Stolz, "The Nursery Comes to the Shipyard" *New York Times Magazine*, November 7, 1943, p. 39.

60. Miriam Lowenberg, "Shipyard Nursery Schools," *Journal of Home Economics* (February 1944), p. 77.

61. James Hymes, Jr. "The Kaiser Answer: Child Service Centers," *Progressive Education* (May 1944), p. 222.

62. The Kaiser Company, Inc., *Child Service Centers*; *Bo's'n's Whistle*, Oregon Ship, March 10, 1944; *Bo's'n's Whistle*, Swan Island, November 17, 1944; Hymes, "Interview," pp. 50–53.

63. Hymes, "Interview," p. 54, Skold, "Women Workers and Childcare", p. 143.

64. Child Service Department, "The Cost of Operating Child Service Centers," p. 1, Henry J. Kaiser Historical Library; Hymes, "Interview," p. 54.

65. Webb to Anderson, May 15, 1944, Women's Bureau Papers.

66. *Bo's'n's Whistle*, Vancouver, December 22, 1944.

67. Goddard, interview with Skold, May 15, 1976, transcript; Interview #19 with Skold, transcript, and Interview #21 with Skold, June 20, 1976, transcript.

68. Goddard, interview with Skold, transcript, June 15, 1976, p. 23.

69. In September 1944, for example, Mary Keeley of the Child Welfare League of America argued at a meeting of the Oregon Child Care Committee that the large-scale employment of women could have been avoided if manpower in the Portland area had been used more effectively. She also suggested that the reason industrial child-care centers "were established in Portland and not in other places is that local agencies did not get into the program quickly enough" (Minutes, Oregon Child Care Committee, September 13, 1944 Papers of the Oregon Defense Council.)

70. *The Columbian*, April 14, 1944, February 23, 1943, and September 9, 1943.

71. Minutes, Multnomah County Day Care Committee, February 3, 1943.

72. *The Oregonian*, August 22, 1943; Goddard, interview with Skold, transcript.

73. Anderson, *Wartime Women*, p. 133; Richard Polenberg, *War and Society: The United States, 1941–1945* (Philadelphia: Lippincott, 1972), p. 149; Sheila Tropp Lichtman "Women at Work," p. 316.

74. Clawson, *Shipyard Diary*, p. 165.

75. *The Oregonian*, August 21.

76. *The Oregonian*, August 22, 1943.

77. *Voices of American Women*, November 1942, 10; *The Oregonian*, August 27, 1944; "Day Care Facilities in Multnomah County," September 1943, Records of the Portland Council of Social Agencies, TCCC Papers, MSS 1783.

78. Virginia Lemire, Testimony, November 15, 1943, "West Coast Hearings," Records of the Fair Employment Practices Committee, roll #13, microfilm.

79. Hymes, "Interview," p. 49.

80. Interview #20 with Skold, transcript.

81. *The Shipbuilder*, February 1945.

82. Edna Hopkins, interview, May 28, 1981.

83. "Kaiser's Children," *Survey Mid-Monthly, Journal of Social Work* 80 (December 1944): 351.

84. *Bo's'n's Whistle*, Swan Island, November 10, 1944; Hymes, "Interview" pp. 48–49; Skold, "Women Workers and Childcare," pp. 146–47, 174–77; The Kaiser Company, Inc., *Kaiser Child Service Centers*.

85. Minutes, Oregon Child Care Committee, June 16, 1943 Papers of the Oregon Defense Council.

86. *The Oregonian*, May 21, 1944 and June 20, 1944.

87. Nell Conley, interview, April 3, 1981.

88. Interview #21, with Skold, transcript.

89. Jerold Owen to Saidie Dunbar, December 18, 1943, Papers of the Oregon State Defense Council.

90. *Bo's'n's Whistle*, Vancouver, July 11, 1944.

91. James Hymes, Jr., "The Kaiser Answer: Child Service Centers," *Progressive Education*, May, 1944, p. 246.

92. Two articles on the Kaiser centers appeared in the 1970s: Carol Slobodin, "When the U.S. Paid for Day Care," *Day Care and Early Education*, September–October 1975, 22–25, and Belle Canon, "The Kaiser Shipyard Experiment of World War II, A Forgotten Revolution in Child Care," *Oregon Times Magazine*, February–March 1976, 21–24. The James Hymes interview with Lois Stolz was released as a sound recording in 1972.

Chapter Four

1. Two works, both unpublished, which discuss the wartime debate on women's postwar future are Josephine Chandler Holcomb, "Women in the Labor Force in the United States, 1940–1950" (Ph.D. dissertation, University of South Carolina, 1976), and Eleanor Straub, "Government Policy Toward Civilian Women during World War II" (Ph.D. dissertation, Emory Univrsity, 1973).

2. Edward P. Thompson, *The Making of the English Working Class* (New York: Pantheon, 1964), p. 12; Ferdinand Braudel cited in Herbert Gutman, *Work, Culture and Society in Industrializing America: Essays in American Working-Class and Social History* (New York: Knopf, 1976), p. 67.

3. Nell Giles, "What About the Women: Do They Want to Keep Their Factory Jobs when the War's Over?" *Ladies' Home Journal*, June 1944, p. 22.

4. *The New York Times*, August 16, 1943.

5. Karl T. Schlotterbeck, *Postwar Employment: The Magnitude of the Problem*, Pamphlet No. 54, (Washington, D.C.: The Brookings Institution, 1943), p. 13.

6. Cynthia Harrison, *On Account of Sex: The Politics of Women's Issues 1945–68* (Berkeley: University of California Press, 1988), p. 7. The groups that were most active in promoting women's interests during the war were the Women's Bureau, the Women's Trade Union League, the International Labour Organization, the Russell Sage Foundation, the National Federation of Business and Professional Women's Clubs, and the Women's Advisory Committee of the War Manpower Commission. The period during and immediately after World War II represents in many ways the last gasp of activism on behalf of women for several of these groups. After the war they

either expired or experienced shifts in leadership and direction that made them less aggressive advocates for women. The Women's Trade Union League went out of existence in 1950; the National Federation of Business and Professional Women's Clubs changed the name of its journal from *The Independent Woman* to *National Business Woman* in 1956. While the Women's Bureau survived after its absorption into the Division of Labor Statistics in 1954, its staff was dispersed and its autonomy reduced. (Judith Sealander, *As Minority Becomes Majority: Federal Reaction to the Phenomenon of Women in the Work Force, 1920–1963* [Westport, Conn.: Greenwood, 1983] chapter 7.) In 1959, Mary Anderson wrote to Mary Van Kleeck complaining that the Women's Bureau "does nothing for women in industry" (Anderson to Van Kleeck, April 12, 1959, Mary Van Kleeck Papers, Box 9, Smith College).

7. See, for example, Straub, p. 3.

8. "History of the WAC," p. 7, Women's Bureau Papers, U.S. Department of Labor, RG 86, Box 1561, National Archives (hereafter cited as NA); International Labour Office, *The War and Women's Employment* (Montreal: International Labour Office, 1946), p. 275; Bryn Mawr College, Carola Woerishoffer Graduate Department of Social Economy and Social Research, *Women during the War and After: Summary of a Comprehensive Study* (New York: Curtis, 1945); Postwar Planning Document, p. 4, Women's Bureau Papers RG 86, Box 1561.

9. "Equal Pay for Women Workers," *Monthly Labor Review* 63 (September 1946), pp. 380–389.

10. Theresa Wolfson, "Aprons and Overalls in War," *Annals of the American Academy of Political and Social Science* 229 (September 1943), p. 55.

11. See, for example, Mary Anderson, "The Post-War Role of American Women," *American Economic Review* 34 (March 1944), p. 243; National Women's Trade Union League (hereafter cited as NWTUL) of America, *Action Needed! Post-War Jobs for Women* (Washington, D.C.: National Women's Trade Union League, 1944), p. 22.

12. Anderson, "The Post-War Role of American Women," p. 245.

13. Sealander, p. 105.

14. U.S. Department of Labor, Women's Bureau, *Women Workers in Ten War Production Areas and Their Postwar Employment Plans*, Bulletin No. 209 (Washington, D.C.: Government Printing Office, 1946).

15. See, for example, Anderson, "The Post-War Role of American Women"; NWTUL, *Action Needed!* Disagreements among women's groups about the most effective method of protecting the postwar rights of women in the work force echoed the prewar debate about the equal rights amendment, which continued to divide women's groups throughout the war. The coalition

of groups that supported the ERA had grown since the New Deal but still excluded most organizations concerned with the problems of women wage earners. ERA advocates saw a constitutional amendment as a more effective strategy for protecting the postwar rights of women workers than either state or federal equal-pay laws, which they contended would be unnecessary if the amendment were passed. Some of the pro-ERA groups, notably the Women's Party, actively opposed equal-pay laws because they saw them as a "way of admitting that where your economic market is unregulated, uncontrolled, women cannot get the same wages for their labors and for their services, even though it is comparable to the work of men in both quality and production." Rebecca S. Greathouse, "The Effect of Constitutional Equality on Working Women," *American Economic Review* 34 (March 1944); Quote from Blanche Friedman, testimony, "Hearings on the Equal Rights Amendment," Senate Subcommittee on the Judiciary, September 28, 1945, p. 100. For a discussion of the postwar argument about the Equal Rights Amendment see Cynthia Harrison, *On Account of Sex*, Chapter 1.

16. U.S. Dept. of Labor, Women's Bureau Papers, RG 86, Box 1561. The General Federation of Women's Clubs established a Post-War Planning Department whose objective was "to see that qualified women serve as members of each community, county, and state groups [*sic*] which are studying and developing plans for the postwar period" (Oregon Federation of Women's Clubs, Manual, 1945–46); Mary Van Kleeck of the Russell Sage Foundation worked to establish local community councils for employment and development and urged women to become involved in these councils by using the social housekeeping arguments of the prewar period. "Managing a community," she told the Mothers Service Club of New Brunswick, New Jersey, "is not very different from managing a home on a larger scale" (Mary Van Kleeck Papers, Box 24, Smith College). The Women's Trade Union League succeeded in getting Agnes Nestor appointed as their representative to the AFL postwar planning committee but the victory was a hollow one because she was unable to have much influence.

17. A. Browning, "Will There Be a Job for Mrs. Jones?" *Christian Science Monitor Magazine*, June 1945, p. 3.

18. Giles, p. 161.

19. Giles, p. 23.

20. Robert Moses, *Portland Improvement* (New York: November 10, 1943), p. 19.

21. Untitled typescript, p. 1, Portland Planning Bureau Files, City of Portland Archives; Moses, p. 19.

22. "Detour through Purgatory," *Fortune*, February 1945, p. 181.

23. "Description of the Portland Area Postwar Development Commission," (hereafter called PAPDC) William Bowes Papers, MSS 1372, Box 2, Oregon Historical Society (hereafter cited as OHS). Vancouver organized its postwar planning group in June, 1943; *The Columbian*, June 22, 1943.

24. "Description of the PAPDC," Bowes Papers.

25. E. Kimbark MacColl, *The Growth of a City: Power and Politics in Portland, Oregon, 1915 to 1950* (Portland, Oreg.: Georgian, 1979), p. 585.

26. *The Oregon Club Woman*, vol. 29, no. 1 (October–November 1942), p. 10. The 1945–46 Manual of the Oregon Federation of Women's Clubs urged women to get involved in postwar committees on a local level.

27. *The Oregonian*, 1941–1945; Saidie Dunbar's diary also refers to many women involved in wartime organizing in Portland (Saidie Dunbar Papers, Ax 26, University of Oregon).

28. *Bo's'n's Whistle*, Vancouver, May 19, 1944.

29. *Bo's'n's Whistle*, Swan Island, May 26, 1944.

30. *Bo's'n's Whistle*, Vancouver, August 19, 1944; see *Bo's'n's Whistle*, Oregon Ship, May 26, 1944, *Bo's'n's Whistle*, Vancouver, June 2, 1944, and *Bo's'n's Whistle*, Swan Island, June 9, 1944, for pleas to workers to remain on the job.

31. Oregon Unemployment Compensation Commission, "Study of the Solvency of the Oregon Unemployment Compensation Trust Fund," City of Portland, Planning Files, Box 20, Post-War Employment folder, City of Portland Archives.

32. *Christian Science Monitor Magazine*, June 2, 1945.

33. *The People's Observer*, 1943–1945.

34. "Description of the PAPDC," Bowes Papers.

35. MacColl, p. 587.

36. Robert Moses reported that he had originally been asked to design an even larger project than he did (Robert Moses, *Working for the People* [New York: Harper and Brothers, 1956], p. 235).

37. Moses, *Portland Improvement*, p. 19.

38. Ibid. p. 10.

39. *The New York Times*, October 31, 1943.

40. *The Oregonian*, April 17, 1943; February 19, 1944.

41. Ruth Drurey, April 18, 1981 and Dorothy Anderson, May 22, 1981, interviews.

42. *The Oregonian*, November 21, 1943.

43. *The Oregonian*, November 21, 1943.

44. PAPDC, "Shipyard Survey," summary tables, p. 1, Portland Planning Files, Box 20; sample questionnaire, Records of the U.S. Maritime Commission, RG 178, Box 415, NA.

45. "Shipyard Survey," summary tables, Portland Planning Files.

46. The figure for office workers is approximate because it includes office and no response," Portland Committee on Postwar Planning, "Shipyard Survey," summary tables, Portland Planning Files; sample questionnaire.

47. Portland Committee on Postwar Planning, "Shipyard Survey," summary tables, p. 5, Portland Planning Files; *Bo's'n's Whistle*, Oregon Ship, December 8, 1944.

48. Portland Committee on Postwar Planning, "Shipyard Survey," summary tables, Portland Planning Files, p. 5.

49. *The Columbian*, March 8, 1944.

50. *Bo's'n's Whistle*, Oregon Ship, March 10, 1944.

51. *Bo's'n's Whistle*, Vancouver, September 29, 1944; see also *Bo's'n's Whistle*, Oregon Ship, September 22, 1944; *Bo's'n's Whistle*, Oregon Ship, October 27, 1944.

52. *Bo's'n's Whistle*, Oregon Ship, March 10, 1944; "Shipyard Survey," Oregon Shipbuilding Corporation Tables, Portland Planning Files.

53. Nell Conley, interview, April 3, 1981.

54. Loena Ellis, interview, May 15, 1981.

55. Etta Harvey, interview, May 28, 1981.

56. Nona Pool, interview, May 25, 1981.

57. Jean Clark, interview, June 2, 1981.

58. *Bo's'n's Whistle*, Swan Island, July 21, 1944.

59. *Bo's'n's Whistle*, Vancouver, April 20, 1945.

60. *Bo's'n's Whistle*, Oregon Ship, July 28, 1944.

Chapter 5

1. Lisa Anderson and Sheila Tobias "What Really Happened to Rosie the Riveter? Demobilization and the Female Labor Force, 1944–47," New York: MSS Modular Publications, 1974), p. 1.

2. Alan Clive, "Women Workers in World War II: Michigan as a Test Case," *Labor History* 20 (1979), pp. 46–71; Carl Degler, *At Odds: Women and*

the Family in America from the Revolution to the Present (New York: Oxford University Press, 1980), p. 434; D'Ann Campbell, *Women at War with America: Private Lives in a Patriotic Era* (Cambridge, Mass.: Harvard University Press, 1984).

3. Nancy Gabin, "Women Workers in the UAW in the Post–World War II Period," *Labor History* 21 (Winter 1980), p. 16.

4. See for example, Gabin, Tobias, Anderson, and Lynn Goldfarb, *Separated and Unequal: Discrimination against Women Workers after World War II* (Washington, D.C.: Union for Radical Political Economics, n.d.)

5. *Business Week*, November 24, 1945, p. 94.

6. U.S. Department of Labor, Bureau of Labor Statistics, Employment Statistics Division, *Women in Factories – October 1939 to December 1945* (Washington, D.C.: Government Printing Office, March 1946), pp. 3, 1; *Business Week*, November 24, 1945, p. 96.

7. Quotes from *Business Week*, November 24, 1945, p. 92; U.S. Department of Labor, Women's Bureau, *Women Workers after VJ Day in One Community, Bridgeport, Connecticut*, Bulletin No. 216 (Washington, D.C.: Government Printing Office, 1946), p. 10.

8. *Business Week*, December 29, 1945, 96, 99.

9. Mary Waggaman, *Women Workers in Wartime and Reconversion* (New York: Paulist Press, 1947), pp. 9, 18.

10. *Business Week*, December 19, 1945, p. 92; quote in *Business Week*, November 24, 1945, p. 96; *Monthly Labor Review*, June 1946, pp. 930–31.

11. *Business Week*, November 24, 1945, p. 96.

12. *Monthly Labor Review*, March 1947, p. 416.

13. *Monthly Labor Review*, November 1946, p. 678; U.S. Dept. of Labor, Women's Bureau, *Women Workers after VJ Day*, p. 26.

14. Paddy Quick, "Rosie the Riveter, Myths and Realities," *Radical America* 9 (July–August 1975), p. 199.

15. "Postwar Readjustment and Development Commission Progress Report," p. 1, William Bowes Papers, MSS 1372, Oregon Historical Society (hereafter cited as OHS); Diary of Saidie Dunbar, February 12, 1945, Saidie Dunbar Papers, Ax 26, University of Oregon.

16. *Bo's'n's Whistle*, Swan Island, February 2, 1945; "Postwar Readjustment and Development Commission Progress Report," p. 4, Bowes Papers.

17. "Postwar Readjustment and Development Commission of Oregon Progress Report," p. 4, Bowes Papers.

18. *Bo's'n's Whistle*, Swan Island, March 23, 1945.

19. "Labor Market Bulletin," June, 1945, p. 2, United States Employment Service (hereafter cited as USES) Records, RG 183, Box 304, National Archives (hereafter cited as NA).

20. Nona Pool, "Shipyard Diary," May 4, 1943, possession of author; Nona Pool personal letter to the author, December 10, 1983, possession of the author.

21. *Bo's'n's Whistle*, Vancouver, May 11, 1945.

22. Ibid.

23. Minutes, Multnomah County Day Care Committee, June 12, 1945, Records of the Portland Council of Social Agencies, Tri-County Community Council (hereafter cited as TCCC) Records, MSS 1783, OHS; Dorothy Newman, *Employing Women in the Shipyards*, Department of Labor, Women's Bureau (Washington, D.C.: Government Printing Office, 1944), pp. 19–20; "Postwar Readjustment and Redevelopment Commission Progress Report," June 1945, p. 4, Bowes Papers. See Deborah Ann Hirschfield, "Rosie Also Welded: Women and Technology in Shipbuilding during World War II" (Ph.D. dissertation, University of California at Irvine, 1987), p. 211, for a discussion of ship repair in the shipbuilding industry.

24. Minutes, Multnomah County Day Care Committee, August 22, 1945, Records of the Portland Council of Social Agencies, TCCC Records.

25. "Trend of Employment in Reporting Establishments, Portland, Oregon," September 1945, USES Records.

26. Virginia Larson, interview, April 12, 1981.

27. Mabel Studebaker, interview, April 15, 1981.

28. Edna Hopkins, interview, May 28, 1981.

29. Virginia Larson, interview, April 17, 1981.

30. Ibid.

31. Nona Pool, interview, May 25, 1981.

32. Nell Conley, interview, April 3, 1981.

33. LueRayne Culbertson, interview, May 4, 1981.

34. Reva Baker, interview, April 24, 1981.

35. Loena Ellis, interview, May 15, 1981.

36. Betty Cleator, interview, June 6, 1981.

37. Jean Clark, interview, June 2, 1981.

38. Marie Schreiber, interview, May 17, 1981.

39. *Bo's'n's Whistle,* August 24, 1945; Oregon Labor Market Information, January 1947, USES Records; Margaret Kay Anderson to Frieda Miller, November 19, 1946, U.S. Department of Labor, Women's Bureau Papers, RG 86, Box 1410, NA; Edna Hopkins, interview, May 28, 1981; Betty Niederhaus, interview, May 17, 1981; Marie Schreiber, interview, May 17, 1981; Patricia Koehler, interview, June 6, 1981.

40. Nell Conley, interview, April 3, 1981.

41. Mabel Studebaker, interview, April 15, 1981.

42. *Commerce,* September 17, 1946 and March 13, 1946.

43. Edna Hopkins, interview, May 28, 1981.

44. "Field Report," January 1946, U.S. Dept. of Labor, USES Records, RG 183, Box 304, NA.

45. See USES Field Reports, USES Records, January 1945 through May 1947. Lois Helmbold has pointed out that as the labor market grew tighter during the Depression, sexual attractiveness became a more important requirement for many clerical and service jobs. While this doesn't appear explicitly in the USES reports, it was implied by the age requirement. Lois Rita Helmbold, "Downward Occupational Mobility during the Great Depression: Urban Black and White Working Women," *Labor History* (Spring 1988), p. 150.

46. Margaret Kay Anderson to Frieda Miller, November 19, 1946, U.S. Dept. of Labor, Women's Bureau Papers, RG 86, Box 1410, NA.

47. See, for example, "Reconversion Experiences of Northwest Shipyard Workers," *Monthly Labor Review* (March 1947), pp. 627–35, for a study of four hundred shipyard workers in Vancouver and Tacoma.

48. Margaret Kay Anderson to Frieda Miller, November 19, 1946, U.S. Dept. of Labor, Women's Bureau Papers, RG 86, Box 1410, NA.

49. Helmbold, pp. 135–72.

50. Helmbold, p. 138.

51. Margaret Kay Anderson to Frieda Miller, November 19, 1946, U.S. Dept. of Labor, Women's Bureau Papers.

52. Ibid.

53. Quote in Margaret Kay Anderson to Frieda Miller, November 19, 1946, U.S. Department of Labor, Women's Bureau, *Changes in Women's Employment during the War*, Special Bulletin No. 20 (Washington, D.C.: Government Printing Office, 1944), p. 23.

54. Oregon State Unemployment Compensation Commission, "Reports" January 1948, U.S. Dept. of Labor, USES Records, Box 305.

55. Oregon State Unemployment Compensation Commission, "Reports," May 1947, U.S. Dept. of Labor, USES Records, Box 305.

56. Portland-Vancouver Unemployment Bulletin, December 1948, U.S. Dept. of Labor, USES Records, Box 305.

57. Portland-Vancouver Area, Year Report, December 1948 USES Records, Box 305.

58. Postwar Readjustment and Development Commission, "Progress Report", July 1947, p. 3, Bowes Papers.

59. Marie Schreiber, interview, May 17, 1981.

60. Kathryn Blair, interview, April 26, 1981.

61. Dorothy Anderson, interview, May 22, 1981; Ruth Drurey, interview, April 18, 1981.

62. Katherine Baker, interview, April 4, 1981.

63. Ibid.

64. Betty Cleator, interview, June 6, 1981.

65. Loena Ellis, interview, May 15, 1981.

66. Virginia Larson, interview, April 12, 1981.

67. Marie Schreiber, interview, May 17, 1981.

68. Margaret Kay Anderson to Frieda Miller, November 19, 1946, U.S. Dept. of Labor, Women's Bureau Papers.

69. Pat Rowlands, interview, May 20, 1981.

70. Betty Niederhaus May 17, 1981, Virginia Larson April 12, 1981 and Edna Hopkins May 18, 1981 interviews.

71. Audrey Moore, interview, June 15, 1981.

72. Marie Merchant, interview, June 20, 1981.

73. Margaret Kay Anderson to Frieda Miller, November 19, 1946, Women's Bureau Records, Box 1410; Beatrice Marshall, interview, June 11, 1981.

74. Peter Filene, *Him/Her Self: Sex Roles in Modern America* (New York: Harcourt Brace Jovanovich, 1975), p. 169.

75. "Kaiser's Children," *Survey Mid-Monthly* 80, (1944), p. 351.

76. David Levy, "The War and Family Life," *American Journal of Orthopsychiatry* 15 (1945), pp. 140.

77. Levy, p. 152.

78. Alice Dashiell, "Day Care of Children," *Social Work Yearbook*, 1947, p. 147.

79. *Bo's'n's Whistle*, August 24, 1945.

80. Minutes, Oregon Child Care Committee (then called Oregon Advisory Committee on Child Care, Health and Welfare), January 27, 1943 Papers of the Oregon Defense Council – Oregon State Archives.

81. Minutes, Multnomah County Day Care Committee, June 12, 1945, Records of the Portland Council of Social Agencies, TCC Records.

82. Minutes, Multnomah County Day Care Committee, August 28, 1945, Records of the Portland Council of Social Agencies TCCC Records.

83. For example, see letters to Clyde Doyle, congressman from California, in *Congressional Record*, 795h Cong. 1st sess., vol 91, p. A4076.

84. For the role of the CIO women's auxiliaries, see columns by Eleanor Fowler in *CIO News*, May 1945 to March 1946. The earliest record of organizing in the Portland-Vancouver Area to extend Lanham Act funds was a phone call from Natalie Panek to Saidie Dunbar in May (Diary of Saidie Dunbar, May 17, 1945, Saidie Dunbar Papers); *The Columbian*, August 29, 1945; Minutes, Multnomah County Day Care Committee, June–September 1945, Records of the Portland Council of Social Agencies, TCCC Records; Lillian Herstein to Phil Brady, September 6, 1945, Records of the Portland Council of Social Agencies, TCCC Records; Memorandum, August 30, 1945, Labor Temple Papers, Mss 1401, OHS; Minutes, Multnomah County Day Care Committee, September 11, 1945, Records of the Portland Council of Social Agencies, TCCC Records.

85. Diary of Saidie Dunbar, May 17, 1945, Saidie Dunbar Papers; *The Columbian*, August 29, 1945; Minutes, Multnomah County Day Care Committee, June–September 1945; Lillian Herstein to Phil Brady, September 6, 1945, Records of the Portland Council of Social Agencies, TCCC Records, MSS 1788; Memorandum, August 30, 1945, Labor Temple Papers, MSS 140.

86. See for example Minutes, Multnomah County Day Care Committee, August 22, 1945, and October 9, 1945 Records of the Portland Council of Social Agencies, TCC Records.

87. The Oregon campaign was not unique in its focus on servicemen's wives. See letters from California in *Congressional Record*, 79th Cong., 1st sess., vol. 91, pp. A4155 and A4156.

88. Multnomah County Day Care Committee, October 9, 1945, January, 1946 Records of the Portland Council of Social Agencies, TCCC Records.

89. Minutes, Multnomah County Day Care Committee, September 11, 1945 Records of the Portland Council of Social Agencies, TCCC Records.

90. Minutes, Multnomah County Day Care Committee, October 9, 1945 Records of the Portland Council of Social Agencies, TCC Records.

91. Alice Dashiell, "Day Care of Children," *Social Work Yearbook*, 1947, p. 147; *CIO News*, September 3, 1945.

92. Howard Dratch, "The Politics of Child Care in the 1940s," *Science and Society* 38 (Summer 1974), pp. 167–204.

93. *CIO News*, March 4, 1945 p. 13. The Child Welfare League, for example, was asking for funds to be extended until June 1946.

94. Minutes, Multnomah County Day Care Committee, October 1945–April 1946, Records of the Portland Council of Social Agencies, TCCC Records; *The Columbian*, October 1945–April 1946.

95. Minutes, Multnomah County Day Care Committee, March 26, 1946 Records of the Portland Council of Social Agencies, TCCC Records.

96. Minutes, Multnomah County Day Care Committee, November 28, 1945 Records of the Portland Council of Social Agencies, TCCC Records.

97. "Statement of Need," July 1946, "Report on Day Care Agencies 1945–1946"; and Minutes, March 1946: Multnomah County Day Care Committee, Records of the Portland Council of Social Agencies, TCCC Records.

98. These surveys were conducted by a group called "The Day Care Committee," "Statements of Need for Day Care of Children of Working Mothers in Lanham Fund Nurseries and Extended School Services and Recommended Budget," Records of the Portland Council of Social Agencies, TCCC Records.

99. Minutes, Multnomah Day Care Committee, April 23, 1946 Records of the Portland Council of Social Agencies, TCCC Records.

100. *Bo's'n's Whistle*, September 1, 1945.

101. Quoted in Amy Kesselman, Tina Tau, and Karen Wickre, "Good Work, Sister! The Making of an Oral History Production," *Frontiers: A Journal of Women's Studies* 7, no. 1 (1983), p. 70.

102. LueRayne Culbertson, interview, May 4, 1981.

103. U.S. Bureau of the Census, 16th Decennial Census, *Characteristics of the Population*, vol. 2, part 5, p. 1047 and part 7, G.P.O. , 1943 p. 398; 17th Decennial Census, *Characteristics of the Population*, vol. II, part 37, p. 51 and part 47, GPO, 1952 p. 63.

104. The percentage of women working for wages in Vancouver rose from 25.6 percent in 1940 to 31 percent in 1950; in the city of Portland it rose from 27 percent in 1940 to 32 percent in 1950, U.S. Bureau of the Census, 16th Decennial Census, *Characteristics of the Population*, vol. 2, part 5, p. 1001 and Part 7, p. 398; 17th Decennial Census, vol. 2, part 37, p. 75 and part 47, p. 63; Gertrude Bancroft, *The American Labor Force: Its Growth and Changing Composition* (New York: Wiley, 1958), pp. 70, 216.

105. Bancroft, p. 226. Since the census reports marital status of workers only for cities of over 100,000, figures were not available for Vancouver.

106. U.S. Bureau of the Census, 17th Decennial Census, vol. II, *Characteristics of the Population* part 37, p. 155. Carl Degler, in *At Odds* p. 423, notes that in 1950 the number of women welders in the country as a whole was four and a half times larger than it had been in 1940 and that therefore opportunities for women widened in the postwar period. This figure is extremely misleading when we consider that the numbers were very small in 1940 while the number of women workers who were trained in this craft had increased so markedly during the war. In Multnomah County (which includes Portland), for example, the number of women in industrial crafts almost doubled from 1940 to 1950, growing from 409 to 846, but these women remained only 1 percent of the female workforce, and their percentage of all craftsmen grew only from 2.5 to 3 percent. When one considers that there were over 20,000 women working in industrial crafts during the war, these figures do not indicate much of an advance. According to wartime surveys, well over nine thousand female industrial workers in the Kaiser shipyards alone wanted to continue in their wartime trades, and under a thousand women could be found doing industrial work in 1950. To the thousands of women unable to use their skills in the postwar world, the opportunities had not "widened enormously"; they had narrowed drastically.

107. U.S. Bureau of the Census 16th Decennial Census, vol. II, *Characteristics of the Population* part 5, p. 967; 17th Decennial Census, vol. II, part 37, pp. 140, 146.

108. U.S. Bureau of the Census 16th Decennial Census, vol. II, *Characteristics of the Population* part 5, p. 398; 17th Decennial Census, vol. 2, part 47, p. 67.

109. U.S. Bureau of the Census 16th Decennial Census, vol. II, *Characteristics of the Population* part 7, p. 968; 17th Decennial Census, vol. 2, part 37, pp. 140, 134 and part 47, p. 73; Bancroft, p. 86.

110. U.S. Bureau of the Census 17th Decennial Census, vol. II, *Characteristics of the Population* part 37, p. 137. Myra Marx Ferree has suggested that reliance on younger female labor conceals the lack of mobility in clerical work since younger women tend to move in and out of the work force during childbearing years (personal conversation).

111. Alice Kessler-Harris, *Out to Work: A History of Wage-Earning Women in the United States*, (New York: Oxford University Press, 1982) p. 322.

112. Edna Hopkins, interview, May 28, 1981.

113. Pat Rowlands, interview, May 20, 1981.

114. Betty Niederhaus, interview, May 17, 1981.

115. U.S. Bureau of the Census, 17th Decennial Census, Vol. II *Characteristics of the Population*, Part 37 p. 137; Bancroft, 226.

116. See, for example, *The Oregonian*, August 3, 1945.

117. Betty Niederhaus, interview, May 17, 1981.

118. Sherna Gluck, *Rosie the Riveter Revisited, Women, the War and Social Change*, Boston: G.K.-Hall, 1987, 267.

119. Larson, Hudlicky, Ellis, Drurey, Anderson, Niederhaus, Cleator, Clark, and Conley all mentioned that they would have been interested in working in some form of skilled industrial trade.

120. Nona Pool, interview, May 25, 1981.

121. Ibid.

122. Ibid.

123. Bancroft, p. 58.

124. Reva Baker, interview, April 24, 1981.

125. Katherine Baker, interview, April 14, 1981.

126. Ibid.

127. Nona Pool, interview, May 25, 1981.

128. See, for example, Maureen Honey, *Creating Rosie the Riveter: Class, Gender and Propaganda during World War II* (Amherst: University of Massachusetts Press, 1984), and Susan Hartmann, *The Home Front and Beyond: American Women in the 1940s* (Boston: Twayne, 1982).

129. See *The Oregonian, The Columbian,* and *The Oregon Labor Press* for local attitudes; see Karen Anderson, *Wartime Women: Sex Roles, Family Relations, and the Status of Women during World War II* (Westport, Conn.:

Greenwood, 1981), chapter 3, and Susan Hartmann, *The Home Front and Beyond*, chapter 5, for a national overview of the attitudes toward women and the family.

130. Loena Ellis, interview, May 15, 1981.

131. Hirschfield, "Rosie Also Welded," pp. 233–40.

132. Berenice Thompson, interview, November 20, 1980.

133. Patricia Koehler, interview, June 6, 1981.

134. Kathryn Blair, interview, April 26, 1981.

SELECTED REFERENCES

Books and Pamphlets

Anderson, Karen. Wartime Women: Sex Roles, Family Relations, and the Status of Women during World War II. Westport, Conn.: Greenwood Press, 1981.

Anderson, Lisa, and Tobias, Sheila. "What Really Happened to Rosie the Riveter? Demobilization and the Female Labor Force, 1944–47." Module 9. New York: MSS Modular Publications, 1974.

Archibald, Katherine. *Wartime Shipyard: A Study in Social Disunity.* Berkeley: University of California Press, 1947.

Baker, Elijah. *Introduction to Steel Shipbuilding.* New York: McGraw Hill, 1953.

Bancroft, Gertrude. *The American Labor Force: Its Growth and Changing Composition.* New York: Wiley 1958. Reprint.

Beechey, Veronica. *Unequal Work.* London: Verso, 1987.

Berch, Bettina. *The Endless Day: The Political Economy of Women and Work.* New York: Harcourt Brace Jovanovich, 1982.

Bryn Mawr College. Carola Woerishoffer Graduate Department of Social Economy and Social Research. *Women during the War and After: Summary of a Comprehensive Study.* New York: Curtis, 1945.

Campbell, D'Ann. *Women at War with America: Private Lives in a Patriotic Era.* Cambridge, Mass.: Harvard University Press, 1984.

Chafe, William H. *The American Woman: Her Changing Social, Economic, and Political Role, 1920–1970.* New York: Oxford University Press, 1972.

169

Child Service Centers. Portland, Oreg.: Oregon Shipbuilding Corporation, the Kaiser Company, 1945.

Clawson, Augusta. *Shipyard Diary of a Woman Welder.* New York: Penguin, 1944.

Degler, Carl N. *At Odds: Women and the Family in America from the Revolution to the Present.* New York: Oxford University Press, 1980.

Easterlin, Richard. *The American Baby Boom in Historical Perspective.* Occasional Paper No. 79. Reprint. New York: National Bureau of Economic Research, 1962.

Elder, Glen. *Children of the Great Depression.* Chicago: University of Chicago Press, 1974.

Farley, Lin. *Sexual Shakedown: Sexual Harassment of Women on the Job.* New York: McGraw-Hill, 1978.

Filene, Peter. *Him/Herself: Sex Roles in Modern America.* New York: Harcourt Brace Jovanovich, 1975.

Flynn, Elizabeth Gurley. *Women in the War.* New York: Workers Library, 1942.

Foner, Philip S. *Women and the American Labor Movement: From the First Trade Unions to the Present.* New York: Free Press (Macmillan), 1979.

Gatlin, Rochelle. *American Women since 1945.* Jackson: University of Mississippi Press, 1987.

Gluck, Sherna Berger. *Rosie the Riveter Revisited: Women, the War and Social Change.* Boston: G. K. Hall, 1987.

Greenwald, Maurine Weiner. *Women, War and Work: The Impact of World War I on Women Workers in the United States.* Westport, Conn.: Greenwood, 1980.

Gregory, Chester. *Women in Defense Work during World War II.* New York: Exposition Press, 1974.

Grele, Ronald J., ed. *Envelopes of South: Six Practitioners Discuss the Method, Theory and Practice of Oral History and Oral Testimony.* Chicago: Precedent, 1975.

Harrison, Cynthia. *On Account of Sex: The Politics of Women's Issues, 1945–68*. Berkeley: University of California Press, 1988.

Hartmann, Susan. *The Home Front and Beyond: American Women in the 1940s*. Boston: G.K. Hall, 1982.

Honey, Maureen. *Creating Rosie the Riveter: Class, Gender and Propaganda during World War II*. Amherst: University of Massachusetts Press, 1984.

International Labour Office. *The War and Women's Employment: The Experience of the United Kingdom and the United States*. Montreal: International Labour Office, 1946.

Jones, Jacqueline. *Labor of Love, Labor of Sorror: Black Women, Work, and the Family from Slavery to the Present*. New York: Random House, 1985.

Kaiser Company, *Child Service Centers*. Portland, Oreg., 1945.

Kaledin, Eugenia. *Mothers and More: Women in the 1950s*. Boston: G. K. Hall, 1984.

Kessler-Harris, Alice. *Out to Work: A History of Wage-Earning Women in the United States*. New York: Oxford University Press, 1982.

Lane, Frederic C. *Ships for Victory: A History of Shipbuilding Under the United States Maritime Commission in World War II*. Baltimore: Johns Hopkins University Press, 1951.

Lingeman, Richard. *Don't You Know There's a War On? The American Home Front, 1941–45*. Toronto: Longmans Canada, 1970.

MacColl, E. Kimbark. *The Growth of a City: Power and Politics in Portland, Oregon, 1915 to 1950*. Portland, Oreg.: Georgian, 1979.

Maben, Manly. *Vanport*. Portland: Oregon Historical Society Press, 1987.

Milkman, Ruth. *Gender at Work: The Dynamics of Job Segregation by Sex during World War II*. Urbana: University of Illinois Press, 1987.

Moses, Robert. *Portland Improvement*. New York: November 10, 1943.

National Foremen's Institute, Inc. *Supervising the Woman War Worker*. Deep River, Conn.: National Foremen's Institute, 1942.

National Industrial Information Committee. *American Women at War*. New York: National Association of Manufacturers, 1942.

National Women's Trade Union League of America. *Action Needed! Post-War Jobs for Women*. Washington, D.C.: National Women's Trade Union League, 1944.

Newman, Dorothy. *Employing Women in the Shipyards*. U.S. Department of Labor, Women's Bureau. Washington, D.C.: Government Printing Office, 1944.

Oppenheimer, Valerie Kincade. *The Female Labor Force in the United States: Demographic and Economic Factors Governing Its Growth and Changing Composition*. Berkeley: Institute of International Studies, 1970.

Oregon State Division of Vocational Education. Descriptive Report of Vocational Training for War Production Workers. Salem, Oreg.: 1945.

Oregon State Public Welfare Commission. *The History of Child Welfare in Oregon*. Portland, Oreg.: Oregon State Public Welfare Commisison, August 1951.

Polenberg, Richard. America at War: The Home Front, 1941–1945. Englewood Cliffs, N.J.: Prentice-Hall, 1968.

———. *War and Society: The United States, 1941–1945*. Philadelphia: Lippincott, 1972.

Rotella, Elyce. *From Home to Office: Women at Work, 1870–1930*. Ann Arbor: Michigan University Press, 1981.

Rupp, Leila J. *Mobilizing Women for War: German and American Propaganda, 1939–1945*. Princeton, N.J.: Princeton University Press, 1978.

Scharf, Lois. *To Work and to Wed: Female Employment, Feminism and the Great Depression*. Westport, Conn.: Greenwood, 1980.

Sealander, Judith. *As Minority Becomes Majority: Federal Reaction to the Phenomenon of Women in the Work Force, 1920–1963*. Westport, Conn.: Greenwood, 1983.

Schlotterbeck, Karl T. *Postwar Employment: The Magnitude of the Problem*. Pamphlet No. 54. Washington, D.C.: The Brookings Institution, 1943.

Seidman, Joel. *American Labor from Defense to Reconversion.* Chicago: University of Chicago Press, 1953.

Sokoloff, Natalie. *Between Money and Love: The Dialectics of Women's Home and Market Work.* New York: Praeger, 1981.

Thomas, Mary Martha. *Riveting and Rationing in Dixie: Alabama Women and the Second World War.* Tuscaloosa: University of Alabama Press, 1987.

U.S. Bureau of Census. Census of Population: 1940, Vol. 2 *Characteristics of the Population,* Part 5. Washington, D.C.: Government Printing Office, 1943.

U.S. Bureau of the Census. Census of Population: 1950, Vol. 4. Special Reports, Part 1. Chapter B, *Occupational Characteristics.* Washington, D.C.: Government Printing Office, 1952.

U.S. Bureau of the Census. Census of Population: 1950, Vol. 2. *Characteristics of the Population,* Part 5. Washington, D.C.: Government Printing Office, 1952.

U.S. Department of Labor, Bureau of Labor Statistics. *Tables of Working Life for Women, 1950* Bulletin No. 1204. Washington, D.C.: Government Printing Office, 1957.

U.S. Department of Labor, Bureau of Labor Statistics, Employment Statistics Division. *Women in Factories – October 1939 to December 1945.* Washington, D.C.: Government Printing Office, March 1946.

——. *Changes in Women's Employment during the War.* Special Bulletin No. 20. Washington, D.C.: Government Printing Office, 1944.

U.S. Department of Labor, Women's Bureau. *Changes in Women's Occupations 1940–1950.* Bulleting No. 253, prepared by Mary Elizabeth Pidgeon. Washington, D.C.: Government Printing Office, 1944.

——. *Differences in the Earnings of Women and Men.* Bulletin No. 152, prepared by Mary Elizabeth Pidgeon. Washington, D.C.: Government Printing Office, 1938.

——. *Employment of Women in the Early Postwar Period, with Background of Prewar and War Data.* Bulletin No. 211, prepared by Mary Elizabeth Pidgeon. Washington, D.C.: Government Printing Office, 1946.

——. *Women in the Economy of the United States of America.* Bulletin No. 155, prepared by Mary Elizabeth Pidgeon. Washington, D.C.: Government Printing Office, 1937.

——. *Women Workers after VJ Day in One Community, Bridgeport, Connecticut.* Bulletin No. 216. Washington, D.C.: Government Printing Office, 1946.

——. *Women Workers in Ten War Production Areas and Their Postwar Employment Plans.* Bulletin No. 209. Washington, D.C.: Government Printing Office, 1946.

U.S. War Manpower Commission. *Survey of Shipyard Operations in the Portland, Oregon, Metropolitan Area.* Vols. 1, 2, and 3. Portland, Oreg.: United States Manpower Commission, 1943.

Waggaman, Mary. *Women Workers in Wartime and Reconversion.* New York: Paulist Press, 1947.

Walsh, Andrea. *Women's Film and Female Experience 1940–1950.* New York: Praeger, 1984.

Wandersee, Winifred D. *Women's Work and Family Values 1920–1940.* Cambridge, Mass.: Harvard University Press, 1981.

Warne, Colston E., ed. "Labor in Post-War America." *Yearbook of American Labor.* Brooklyn: Institute of Labor Studies, Remsen, 1949.

Dissertations and Theses

Herzog, June. "Study of the Negro Defense Workers in the Portland-Vancouver Area." Senior Thesis, Reed College, 1944.

Hirschfield, Deborah Ann. "Rosie Also Welded: Women and Technology in Shipbuilding during World War II." Ph.D. dissertation, University of California at Irvine, 1987.

Holcomb, Joseph Chandler. "Women in the Labor Force in the United States, 1940–1950." Ph.D. dissertation, University of South Carolina, 1976.

Lichtman, Sheila Tropp. "Women at Work, 1941–1945: Wartime Employment in the San Francisco Bay Area." Ph.D. dissertation, University of California at Davis, 1981.

Skold, Karen Beck. "Women Workers and Child Care during World War II: A Case Study of the Portland, Oregon, Shipyards." Ph.D. dissertation, University of Oregon, 1981.

Straub, Eleanor. "Government Policy Toward Civilian Women during World War II." Ph.D. dissertation, Emory University, 1973.

Periodicals

The Boilermakers Journal. Official organ of the International Brotherhood of Boilermakers, Iron Shipbuilders and Helpers of America. 1942–46.

Bo's'n's Whistle. Official Publication of the Kaiser Shipyards, 1941–46.

The Columbian. January 1942 to December 1946.

Commerce. Portland Chamber of Commerce. December 1941 to December 1946.

Flat Top Flash. October 27, 1943 to February 25, 1944.

The Oregon Club Woman. October–November 1941 to April–May 1943.

Oregon Federation of Women's Clubs. *Manual.* 1945–46.

——. *Bulletin.* 1942–45.

——. *Journal.* 1942–45.

Oregon Journal. January 1942 to December 1946.

The Oregon Labor Press. January 1942 to December 1946.

The Oregonian. January 1941 to December 1946.

The People's Observer. June 29, 1943, to February 28, 1945.

The Porthole. Official publication of Commercial Iron Works. July 1944 to September 1945.

The Shipbuilder. Official publication of Local 72 of the International Brotherhood of Boilermakers, Iron Shipbuilders and Helpers of America. May 1942 to March 1945.

Stem to Stern. Official publication of the Willamette Iron and Steel Corporation. 1942–45.

Voice of American Women. 1942–45.

Interviews

A. Northwest Women's History Project

All narrators signed legal release forms permitting the use of the interview material except Beatrice Hadley (pseudonym), who agreed to the use of the material but not the use of her name. The starred tapes are available at the Oregon Historical Society, Portland, Oregon.

Adkins, Ree. Vancouver, Washington, Interview by Lynn Taylor, June 2, 1981.

Anderson, Dorothy. Portland, Oregon, Interview by Amy Kesselman, May 22, 1981.

*Avshalomov, Doris. Portland, Oregon, Interview by Madeline Moore, June 5, 1981.

*Baker, Katherine. Portland, Oregon, Interview by Karen Wikre, April 4, 1981.

Baker, Reva. Lake Oswego, Oregon, Interview by Sandy Polishuk, April 24, 1981.

*Berggren, Helen. Vancouver, Washington, Interview by Lynn Taylor, May 23, 1981.

*Blair, Kathryn. Portland, Oregon, Interview by Madeline Moore, April 26, 1981.

Clark, Jean. Portland, Oregon, Interview by Amy Kesselman, June 2, 1981.

Cleator, Betty. Warrenton, Oregon, Interview by Madeline Moore, June 6, 1981.

*Conley, Nell. Portland, Oregon, Interview by Amy Kesselman and Sarah Cook, April 3, 1981.

Cooper, Frankie. Nashville, Tennessee, Interveiw by member of Rosie the Riveter Film Project, May 20, 1981.

*Culbertson, LueRayne. Gresham, Oregon, May 4, 1981.

Davis, Mabel (Mabel Hegg). Portland, Oregon, Interview by Susan Feldman, May 15, 1981.

*Dickson, Rosa. Portland, Oregon, Interview by Amy Kesselman and Sarah Cook, April 2, 1981.

Drurey, Ruth. Hillsboro, Oregon, Interview by Amy Kesselman, April 18, 1981.

*Ellis, Loena. Portland, Oregon, Interview by Sandy Polishuk, May 15, 1981.

*Erickson, Alice. Portland, Oregon, Interview by Amy Kesselman, June 5, 1981.

Groshong, Eva. Gresham, Oregon, Interview by Amy Kesselman, June 18, 1981.

Hadley, Beatrice [pseudonym]. Gresham, Oregon, Interview by Amy Kesselman, June 5, 1981.

Harvey, Etta. Portland, Oregon, Interview by Sandy Polishuk, May 28, 1981.

*Hopkins, Edna. Vancouver, Washington, Interview by Amy Kesselman, May 28, 1981.

Housman, Lois. Portland, Oregon, Interview by Madeline Moore, May 22, 1981.

*Hudlicky, Joanne. Vancouver, Washington, Interview with Amy Kesselman and Sarah Cook, April 20, 1981.

Koehler, Patricia. Portland, Oregon, Interview by Sarah Cook, June 6, 1981.

Larson, Virginia. Estacada, Oregon, Interview by Madeline Moore, April 22, 1981.

Livesay, Rita. Portland, Oregon, Interview by Amy Kesselman, May 8, 1981.

*Marshall, Beatrice. Portland, Oregon, Interview by Madeline Moore and Chris Poole, June 11, 1981.

Merchant, Marie. Portland, Oregon, Interview by Amy Kesselman, July 20, 1981.

*Moore, Audrey (Audrey Dotsey). Portland, Oregon, Interview by Amy Kesselman, Portland, Oregon, June 15, 1981.

*Niederhaus, Betty, and Schreiber, Marie. Portland, Oregon, Interview by Barbara Wittesly-Hayes, May 17, 1981.

*Pool, Nona. Portland, Oregon, Interview by Amy Kesselman, May 25, 1981.

Rowlands, Pat. Gresham, Oregon, Interview by Karen Wickre, May 20, 1981.

*Strmiska, Billie. Wheeler, Oregon, Interview by Karen Wickre, June 14, 1981.

Studebaker, Mabel. Vancouver, Washington, Interview by Amy Kesselman, April 15, 1981.

*Thompson, Berenice. Gladstone, Oregon, Interview by Amy Kesselman and Sarah Cook, November 20, 1980.

B. *Karen Beck Skold Interviews*

Transcripts for these interviews are located in the Oregon Historical Society, Portland, Oregon.

Interview #4. Teacher at Kaiser Child Service Center.

Interview #13. Elizabeth Goddard, Secretary, Multnomah Day Care Committee, May 13, 1976.

Interview #15. Cornella Novak, Coordinator of Lanham-Funded public school nurseries June 12, 1976.

Interview #19 n.d. Head teacher at a Lanham nursery school.

Interview #20. Nurse at Swan Island Child Service Center June 19, 1976.

Interview #21. Teacher at University Homes Child Care Center June 20, 1976.

Interview #24. Teacher at Kaiser Child Service Center July 16, 1976.

Dr. Forrest Rieke, doctor for the Kaiser Shipyards January 9, 1976.

Manuscript Collections

College Park, Maryland: University of Maryland Library. Records of the Industrial Union of Marine and Shipbuilding Workers of America.

Eugene, Oregon: University of Oregon Library. Saidie Dunbar Papers.

Hyde Park, New York: Franklin Delano Roosevelt Library. Eleanor Roosevelt Papers. Correspondence files.

Ithaca, New York: New York State School of Industrial and Labor Relations Archives. Theresa Wolfson Papers.

New Haven, Connecticut. Manuscripts and Archives, Yale University Library. Selected Documents of Records of the Committee on Fair Employment Practice. Microfilm.

Northampton, Massachusetts: Sophia Smith Collection, Smith College, Mary Van Kleeck Papers.

Portland, Oregon: City of Portland Archives. Planning files.

——: Multnomah County Library. Committee on the Day Care of Children of Working Mothers, Report to the Committee on Absenteeism.

——: Oregon Historial Society. Labor Temple Records, 1401.

——: Oregon Historical Society. William Bowes Papers, 1372.

——: Oregon Historical Society. Records of the Portland Council of Social Agencies. Tri-County Community Council Records, 1783.

——: Young Women's Christian Association, Boxes V and XII.

Oakland, California: Henry J. Kaiser Historical Library. Miscellaneous brochures and documents.

Salem, Oregon: Oregon State Archives. Papers of the Defense Council – World War II.

Suitland, Maryland: National Archives. U.S. Maritime Commission Records. RG 178.

——: National Archives. Office of Education Records. RG 12.

Washington, D.C.: National Archives. U.S. Department of Labor, U.S. Employment Service Records. Oregon State Employment Compensation Commission, 1944–48. RG 183.

——: National Archives. U.S. Department of Labor, Women's Bureau Papers. RG 86.

Articles

Alexander, Chester. "National Sex Ratio and the Problem of Reconversion." *School and Society* 61 (June 2, 1945): 362–64.

Allen, Margaret. "The Domestic Ideal and the Mobilization of Womanpower in World War II." *Women's Studies International Forum* 6 (1983): 401–12.

Anderson, Karen. "Last Hired, First Fired: Black Women Workers during World War II." *Journal of American History* 69 (June 1982): 82–97.

Anderson, Mary. "The Post-War Role of American Women." *American Economic Review* 34 (March 1944): 237–44.

Armitage, Sue. "The Next Step." *Frontiers: A Journal of Women's Studies* 7 (1983): 3–8.

Baber, Ray. "Marriage and the Family after the War." *Annals of the American Academy of Political and Social Science* 229 (September 1943): 164–75.

Bland, M. Susan. "Henrietta the Homemaker and Rosie the Riveter: Images of Women in Advertising in MacLean's Magazine 1939–50." *Atlantis* 8 (Spring 1983): 61–86.

Brown, C. "What's Going to Happen to Our Women Workers?" *Good Housekeeping*, December 1943, 42–44.

Browning, A. "Will There Be a Job for Mrs. Jones?" *Christian Science Monitor Magazine*, June 1945, 3.

Campbell, D'Ann. "Was the West Different? Values and Attitudes of Young Women in 1943." *Pacific Historical Review* 17 (August 1978): 453–63.

Canon, Belle. "The Kaiser Shipyard Experiment of World War II: A Forgotten Revolution in Child Care." *Oregon Times*, February–March 1976, 21–24.

Clive, Alan. "Women Workers in World War II: Michigan as a Test Case." *Labor History* 20 (1979): 46–71.

Cuber, John. "Changing Courtship and Marriage Customs." *Annals of the American Academy of Political and Social Science* 299 (September 1943): 30–38.–

Davenal, George. "When Johnny Comes Marching Home: Will You Be March-int Out?" *Independent Woman*, July 1945, 182–83.

Dratch, Howard. "The Politics of Child Care in the 1940s." *Science and Society* 38 (Summer 1974): 167–204.

"Effects of War Casualties on Economic Responsibilities of Women." *Monthly Labor Review* 62 (February 1946): 181–86.

"Employers' Post-War Plans for Women Workers in New York State." *Monthly Labor Review* 60 (July 1945): 1269–1270.

"Employment in the Northwest." *Monthly Labor Review* 64 (April 1947), 589–98.

"Employment in the Shipbuilding Industry, 1939–43." *Monthly Labor Review* 58 (May 1944): 948–59.

"Employment of the Older Worker." *Monthly Labor Review* 62 (March 1946): 392–96.

"Equal Pay for Women Workers." *Monthly Labor Review* 63 (September 1946): 380–89.

"Equal Pay Principle in Union Contracts." *Management Review* 24 (July 1945): 306.

"Extra Workers in the Post-War Labor Force." *Monthly Labor Review* 61 (November 1945): 841–47.

"Factors Determining Post-War Job Transfers and Unemployment." *Monthly Labor Review* 58 (February 1944): 269–77.

Fredricksen, Hazel. "The Program for Day Care of Children of Employed Mothers. *Social Service Review* 17 (June 1945): 159–169.

"The Fortune Survey: Women in America." Part 1, *Fortune*, August 1946, 5; Part 2, *Fortune*, September 1946, 5.

Gabin, Nancy. "They Have Placed a Penalty on Womanhood: The Protest Actions of Women Auto Workers in Detroit Area UAW Locals, 1945–47." *Feminist Studies* 8 (Summer 1982): 373–98.

——. "Women Workers and the UAW in the Post-World War II Period." *Labor History* 21 (Winter 1980): 5–30.

Giles, Nell. "What about the Women: Do They Want to Keep Their Factory Jobs When the War's Over?" *Ladies Home Journal,* June 1944, 22–23, 159, 161.

Gluck, Sherna Berger. "Interlude or Change: Women and the World War II Experience, A Feminist Oral History." *International Journal of Oral History* 3 (June 1982): 93–113.

——. "Women's Oral History, the Second Decade." *Frontiers: A Journal of Women's Studies* 7 (1983): 1–2.-

Greathouse, Rebekah S. "The Effect of Constitutional Equality on Working Women." *American Economic Review* 34 (March 1944): 226–36.

Gross, Edward. "Plus Ça Change . . . the Sexual Structure of Occupations over Time." *Social Problems* 16 (Fall 1968): 198–208.

Hansen, Rhoda Pratt. "I'm Leaving Home Part Time." *Independent Woman,* December 1946, 363–79.

Harris, William. "Federal Intervention in Union Discrimination: The Fair Employment Practices Commission and West Coast Shipyards during World War II." Unpublished paper, Indiana University, 1978.

Hartmann, Heidi. "The Family as the Locus of Gender, Class and Political Struggle: The Example of Housework." *Signs: Journal of Women in Culture and Society* 6 (Spring 1981), 366–94.

Hartmann, Susan. "Prescriptions for Penelope: Literature on Women's Obligations to Returning Veterans." *Women's Studies* 5 (1978): 223–39.

Hoffman, Betty Hannah. "How Much Should They Earn?" *Ladies' Home Journal,* July 1946, 20–23.

Honey, Maureen. "Recruiting Women for War Work: Office of War Information and the Magazine Industry during World War II." Unpublished paper, University of Nebraska, 1980.

——. "The 'Womanpower' Campaign: Advertising and Recruitment Propaganda during World War II." *Frontiers: A Journal of Women's Studies* 6 (1981): 51–56.

——. "The Working-Class Woman and Recruitment Propaganda during World War II: Class Differences in the Portrayal of War Work." *Signs* 8 (Summer 1983): 672–87.

Hymes, James, Jr. "Child-Care Problems of the Night-Shift Mother." *Journal of Consulting Psychology* 8 (1944): 225–28.

——. "The Kaiser Answer. Child Service Centers." *Progressive Education* (May 1944): 222–23, 245–46.

——. "The Kaiser Child Service Centers. An Interview with Lois Meek Stolz." In Hymes, James, ed. *Care of the Children of Working Mothers*, Living History Interviews, Book 2. Carmel, Calif.: Hacienda, 1978.

"Kaiser's Children." *Survey Mid-monthly Journal of Social Work* 80 (December 1944): 351.

Kesselman, Amy; Tau, Tina; and Wickre, Karen. "Good Work, Sister!' The Making of an Oral History Production." *Frontiers: A Journal of Women's Studies* 7 (1983): 64–70.

——. "Hidden Resistance: Women Shipyard Workers after World War II." In Christine Bose et al., eds., *Hidden Aspects of Women's Work*. New York: Praeger, 1987.

Kessler-Harris, Alice. "Equal Opportunity Commission v. Sears Roebuck and Company: A Personal Account." *Radical History Review* 35 (April 1986): 56–79.

——. "Rosie the Riveter: Who Was She?" *Labor History* 24 (Spring 1983): 249–53.

——. "Women's Wage Work as Myth and History." *Labor History* 19 (Spring 1978): 287–307.

"The Labor Force in the First Year of Peace." *Monthly Labor Review* 63 November 1946): 669–80.

Lake, A. "Shipworkers in the Northwest." *American Mercury* (February 1945): 143–51.

Lemisch, Jesse. "Is a Diary a Primary Source? 'Eyewitness Testimony,' Exponential Decay, and Back Transforms; or Some Good News and Bad News from Modern Brain Research with Reference to the Historian's

Use of Reminiscences." Paper presented at the Organization of American Historians Meeting, Los Angeles, California, April 1984.

Levy, David. "The War and Family Life." *American Journal of Orthopsychiatry* 15 (1945): 140–52.

Lowenberg, Miriam. "Shipyard Nursery Schools." *Journal of Home Economics* (February 1944): 75–77.

Lutz, Alma. "Which Road Women Workers? Equal Pay and Special Protective Laws." *Christian Science Monitor Magazine*, February 2, 1946, 2.

Milkman, Ruth. "Organizing the Sexual Division of Labor: Historical Perspectives on 'Women's Work' and the American Labor Movement." *Socialist Review* 10 (January–February 1980): 95–150.

——. "Redefining 'Women's Work': The Sexual Division of Labor in the Auto Industry during World War II." *Feminist Studies* 8 (Summer 1982) 337–72.

——. "Women's Work and the Economic Crisis: Some Lessons Learned from the Great Depression." *Review of Radical Political Economics* 8 (Spring 1976): 73–91, 95–97.

Miller, Frieda. "Postwar Prospects for Women Workers." *Management Review* 34 (March 1945): 84–86.

Nottingham, Elizabeth. "Towards an Analysis of the Effects of Two World Wars on the Role and Status of Middle-Class Women in the English-Speaking World." *American Sociological Review* 12 (December 1947): 666–75.

Ogburn, William Fielding. "Marriages, Births and Divorces." *Annals of the American Academy of Political and Social Science* 229 (September 1943): 20–29.

Palmer, Gladys. "Women in the Post-War Labor Market." *Forum* 104 (October 1945): 130–34.

Pidgeon, Mary. "Women Workers and Recent Economic Change." *Monthly Labor Review* 65 (December 1947): 666–71.

"Postwar Personnel Policies: A Check List." *Management Review* 34 (January 1945): 16–17.

Quick, Paddy. "Rosie the Riveter, Myths and Realities." *Radical America* 9 (July–August 1975): 115–31.

"Recommendation on Separation of Women from Wartime Jobs." *Monthly Labor Review* 61 (September 1945): 506–8.

"Reconversion Experiences of Northwest Shipyard Workers." *Monthly Labor Review* 64 (March 1947) 627–35.

"Rights for Women," *Newsweek*, July 29, 1946, 17.

Riley, Denise. "'The Free Mothers': Pronatalism and Working Women in Industry at the End of Last War in Britain." *History Workshop* 2 (Spring 1981): 59–853.

Rothchild, Mary Aicken. "Using Oral History to find the 'Common Woman,' an Arizona Oral History Project." *Frontiers: A Journal of Women's Studies* 7 (1983): 87–90.

Schloss, Clara, and Polinsky, Ella. "Postwar Labor Turnover among Factory Workers." *Monthly Labor Review* 64 (March 1947): 411–19.

Schweitzer, Mary. "World War II and Female Labor Force Participation Rates." *Journal of Economic History* 40 (March 1980): 81–95.

"Selective Labor." *Business Week*, November 24, 1945, 84–99.

Smith, Harold. "The Problem of Equal Pay for Equal Work in Great Britain during World War II." *Journal of Modern History* 53 (December 1981): 652–72.

Stoddard, Hope. "No Women Being Hired." *Canadian Forum*, June 1946, 58–59.

Stratton, Dorothy. "Women after the War," *Independent Woman*, October 1945, 279–95.

Straub, Eleanor. "U.S. Government Policy toward Civilian Women during World War II." *Prologue* 5 (Winter 1973): 240–54.

Trey, Joan Ellen. "Women in the War Economy: World War II." *Review of Radical Political Economics* 4 (July 1972): 40–57.

Walters, J. E. "Women in Industry." *Annals of the American Academy of Political and Social Science* 229 (September 1943): 57–62.

Warne, Colston E. "Reconversion of Women." *Current History* 8 (March 1945): 200–206.

"Will Prewar Domestic Workers Return?" *Monthly Labor Review* 62 (January f1946): 930–31.

Wolfson, Theresa. "Aprons and Overalls in War." *Annals of the American Academy of Political and Social Science* 229 (September 1943): 46–55.

"Women in the Labor Force," *Business Week*, December 29, 1945, 92–94.

"Women's Bureau Recommends Rate-for-the-Job Principle." *Monthly Labor Review* 62 (February 1946): 230.

"Women's Postwar Job Plans." *Monthly Labor Review* 58 (May 1944): 1030.

Wool, Harold and Pearlman, Lester. "Recent Occupational Trends: Wartime and Postwar Trends Compared: An Appraisal of the Permanence of Recent Movements." *Monthly Labor Review* 65 (August 1947): 139–47.

INDEX